英文

日本 絵 とき事典 7

ILLUSTRATED

A LOOK INTO TOKYO

［東京編］

D1013539

ILLUSTRATED
A LOOK INTO TOKYO

1st edition..............1986
6th edition..............1991

Printed in Japan

About this Book

1) Layout

This book consists of the following three sections
(1) Old Tokyo; (2) Early Modern Tokyo; (3) Present
Day Tokyo.

Each of these sections follows a significant time
period in the evolution of Tokyo. Topics listed in the
feature pages indicate items of cultural interest.

2) Japanese Words

All the Japanese words in this book have been
romanized in accordance with the revised Hepburn
system. Except for the names of places and people, all
Japanese words are printed in italics except where
they appear in headings or bold type. Long vowels are
indicated by a line above, as in *'shintō;* and, since e's
are pronounced "ay" in Japanese, e's at the ends of
words are marked with an acute accent, as in *'saké'*
(pronounced "sahkay").

Dear Readers

   For many people Tokyo evokes the image of a large modern city so westernized as to preclude any attraction worthy of traditional interest. Nothing could be farther from the truth. Tokyo is a city of great cultural contrasts. The evolution of the city through Japanese history bears this out and has been used as the format of this book. Over 120 years ago Tokyo was little more than a castle town which served as the feudal capital of Japan. Today Tokyo is a pulsing, international city that plays host to those attracted to a city with a traditional past and an exciting future. That is the nature of Tokyo where East and West meet. This book is written with a wide selection of places from the old to the new to help you to get to know it much better. We urge you to take advantage of all the descriptions, illustrations and information presented in this book to visit a part of Tokyo which may have never throught existed in a seemingly westernized city.

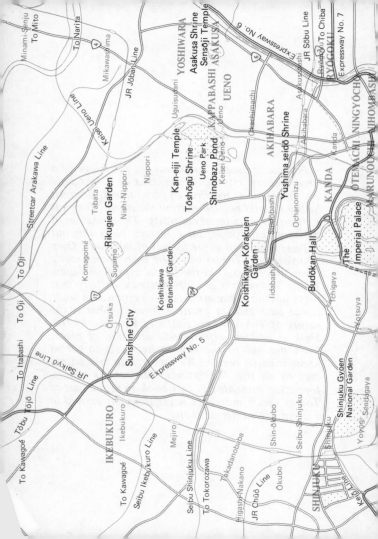

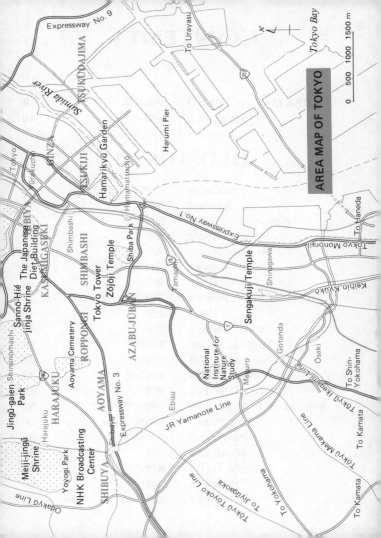

CONTENTS

EARLY MODERN TOKYO

PRESENT DAY TOKYO

USEFUL INFORMATION

FEATURE PAGES

Key to Symbols

 Buildings

 Entertainment

 Urban Districts

 Traditional Arts and Crafts

 Temples and Shrines

 Others

OVERVIEW

Introduction

In this book three stages of Japanese history underlie the section heading categorizing the city of Tokyo. First, "Old Tokyo" describes the colorful atmosphere of the Edo period (1603–1867) found in one part of the city. Next, "Early Modern Tokyo" focuses attention on places reflecting the introduction of western style civilization to Japan at the onset of the Meiji period (1868–1945). Finally, "Present day Tokyo" introduces the showcases of fashion and modern living in this great international city.

Historical Background

Edo, the former name of Tokyo, was derived from Edo Shigenaga, a rising influential figure who acquired this area as a feudal fief at the beginning of 12 C. Afterwards, Edo Castle was founded by Ōta Dōkan at the site of the present day Imperial Palace. In 1590, Edo Castle came under the control of the Edo Shogunate established by Tokugawa Ieyasu, the Supreme Military Commander of Japan. Tokugawa redesigned the city with Edo Castle strategically located in the center. From then on, Edo City served as the administrative center of the nation for a period spanning 300 years. In 1868 succumbing to growing national sentiment and foreign pressure, the Edo shogunate returned the country to Imperial rule. The

Shōgun of that time, Tokugawa Yoshinobu, departed from the city and the castle was handed over without bloodshed. The Emperor who had been living in Kyoto moved to Edo. The city was renamed Tokyo (literally, Eastern Capital) and has served as the capital of Japan ever since.

The introduction of western style civilization first took hold in Tokyo with the adoption of European style architecture in Tsukiji, a residential zone designated for foreigners in the city. Following the lifting of the ban on Christian missionary activities, schools and churches were set up. Western influence on the development of the city expanded. Red brisk paved streets and gas street lights appeared on the Ginza as the first railroad went into service in nearby Shimbashi.

On September 1, 1923, the Great Kantō Earthquake shook through the city of Tokyo. The capital suffered catastrophic damage from the massive force of the 7.9 magnitude tremors and the all consuming fires which followed. Undaunted, the government quickly instituted measures to recover from the disaster. Urban renewal continued. New roads and parks expanded the total area of the city, thus making it the fifth largest in the world. Again, however, the city of Tokyo was reduced to a state of near ruin due to frequent devasting aerial attacks through the course of the Second World War. Postwar recovery moved forward at a suprisingly fast pace closely matched with the rehabilitation of industries. This unparalleled growth shows no sign of slowing down.

The Shitamachi and Yamanoté Sections of the City

Tokyo can be divided into two distinctive sections, Shitamachi and Yamanoté. In a broad sense, the borders of the Shitamachi section are designated by the area between the Yamanoté train line from Tabata Station to Shinagawa Station and the course of the Sumidagawa River. This land at some points is below the level of the adjacent rivers as its name (literally, lower town) indicates. Various expressions of the culture from long ago are abundant in this part of the city providing tourists with an opportunity to experience the traditional life style that flourished in Edo city. In sharp contrast, the Yamanoté section, as its name (literally, "on the mountain side") indicates, has developed on a higher topographical and social level. The trend in the Yamanoté section is toward raising cultural and social awareness by harmonizing western influences to reach new heights in modern thinking and life styles. This concept is reflected in the concentration of large buildings and state of the art facilities in this area. The modern aspects of Tokyo are clearly evident in this urban complex.

The Spirit of the Edokko and other Tokyoites

Ever since the Edo period the character of the contemporary Tokyoite has undergone change from regional Japanese influences. Soon after the establishment of the Tokugawa Shogunate, a culture intrinsically Edo in character developed from the particularly unique temperament of the merchant class who settled here. The original Tokyoite was called "Edokko" (literally, Child of Edo). These people were characterized as easy going in nature, short tempered and open to displays of emotion. They fancied themselves as experts and followers of fashions, food, art. This temperament is often reflected in the main characters of movies and Samurai television programs. Nowadays, however, very few people really fit the description of a true Edokko. The influx of people from the other regions in search of employment and other opportunities has led to a new breed of Tokyoite more individualistic in personality.

OLD TOKYO

asakusa·ueno·nihombashi
ryōgoku·katsushika
taking you back in time

EDO CASTLE

Edo Castle, the residential castle of the *Tokugawa* Shogunate was the center of Japanese politics from 1603 to 1867. Built in 1457 according to the plans of *Ōta Dōkan*, the castle came under the control of *Tokugawa Ieyasu* in 1590. The origin of the present day city of Tokyo stems from the small settlement around the castle which developed into Edo city.

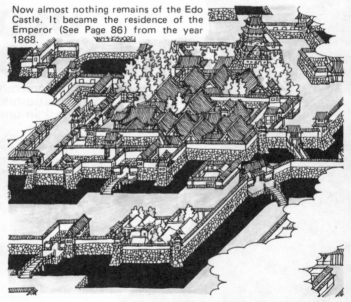

Now almost nothing remains of the Edo Castle. It became the residence of the Emperor (See Page 86) from the year 1868.

Edo Castle was built on an extremely large scale with a 16 km long circumference. A small town adjoining the castle and the mansions of *Daimyō*s, or Feudal Lords were enclosed within this area.

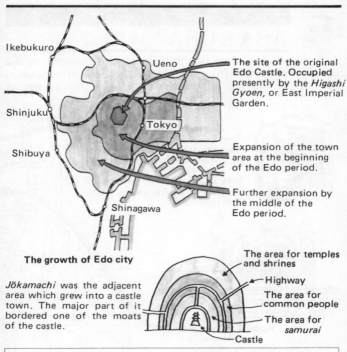

The site of the original Edo Castle. Occupied presently by the *Higashi Gyoen,* or East Imperial Garden.

Expansion of the town area at the beginning of the Edo period.

Further expansion by the middle of the Edo period.

The growth of Edo city

Jōkamachi was the adjacent area which grew into a castle town. The major part of it bordered one of the moats of the castle.

The area for temples and shrines

Highway

The area for common people

The area for *samurai*

Castle

Tokugawa Ieyasu
(1542 – 1616)

The first generation *Shōgun* of a feudal government based in Edo city. He was successful in overcoming all his adversaries in many battles. He established the Edo shogunate which spanned three hundred years of Japanese history.

- 浅草

ASAKUSA

Asakusa was the name of the town which developed around the *Sensōji* Temple from the start of the Edo period. Due in part to the many local theaters and the nearby Yoshiwara

Kaminari 5656 (gorogoro) Hall
Theater performances are held in this colorfully named hall (literally, Rumbling Thunder Hall). Various shops, restaurants and bars in the building provide patrons with a wide variety of leisure activities.

Asakusa Hanayashiki Amusement Park
This park, featuring seasonally blooming flowers and trees, was opened in 1853. However, it has now evolved into a small amusement park with a roller coaster, ghost house and other rides.

The Rokku Area
From the Meiji period (19C) to the start of the Shōwa Reign, the *Asakusa Rokku* (literally, Six Districts) area flourished as an entertainment area attracting people to its operas and light dramatic performances.

Kokusai St.

licensed prostitution quarters, Asakusa quickly grew in importance among the townspeople as the most active of all the commercial areas in Edo city. Although devasted by the end of the Second World War, it has retained a lot of its Edo charm as one of the old downtown neighborhoods visited by scores of sightseers.

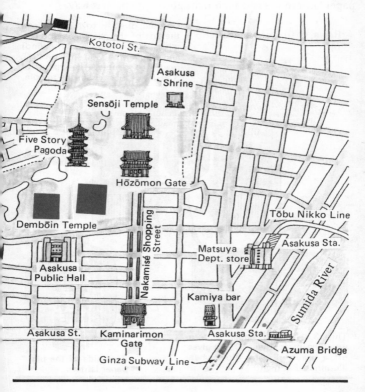

● 雷門

KAMINARIMON GATE

● Ginza Subway Line / 3 min. west of Asakusa Sta.

The main gate leading into the *Sensōji* Temple, *Kaminarimon* is a famous landmark of the Asakusa area itself. A huge red paper lantern is suspended right above the passageway.

Raijin, or God of Thunder

Located directly to the right and the left of the gateway stand two gods, *Fūjin* (the God of Wind) and *Raijin* (the God of Thunder), ready to protect the statue of *Kan-non* enshrined in the temple.

Fūjin, or God of Wind

This 3.3 m red paper lantern weighing more than 100 kg gives off a beautiful warm glow when illuminated at night.

Back side of the big paper lantern

SENSŌJI TEMPLE

• **Ginza Subway Line / 5 min. north of Asakusa Sta.**

The *Sensōji* Temple located in the heart of the Asakusa district, is the oldest temple in all of the metropolitan Tokyo area. According to some accounts the origin of the temple can be traced back to the year 628 when two local fishermen from a nearby district enshrined a small statue of *Kan-non*, the Goddess of Mercy, caught in their fishing net.

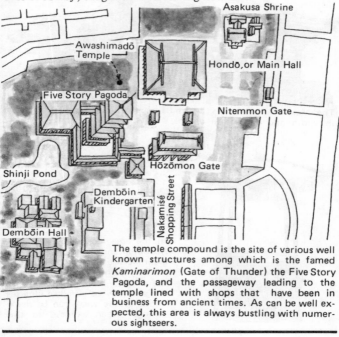

Asakusa Shrine

Awashimadō Temple

Hondō, or Main Hall

Five Story Pagoda

Nitemmon Gate

Shinji Pond

Hōzōmon Gate

Dembōin Kindergarten

Nakamisé Shopping Street

Dembōin Hall

The temple compound is the site of various well known structures among which is the famed *Kaminarimon* (Gate of Thunder) the Five Story Pagoda, and the passageway leading to the temple lined with shops that have been in business from ancient times. As can be well expected, this area is always bustling with numerous sightseers.

Hondō

The original having been destroyed in a fire in the Second World War, the current version of the *Hondō* or the Main Hall of the temple was rebuilt in 1958. The Sacred Statue of *Kan-non*, or the Goddess of Mercy lies preserved in the secret inner sanctum of the large facade of the Main Hall.

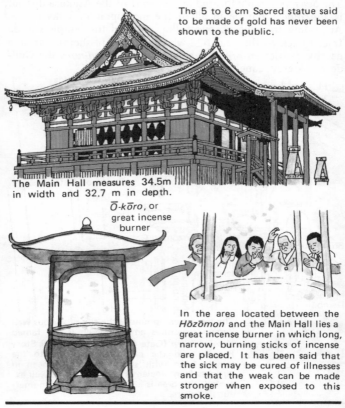

The 5 to 6 cm Sacred statue said to be made of gold has never been shown to the public.

The Main Hall measures 34.5m in width and 32.7 m in depth.

Ō-kōro, or great incense burner

In the area located between the *Hōzōmon* and the Main Hall lies a great incense burner in which long, narrow, burning sticks of incense are placed. It has been said that the sick may be cured of illnesses and that the weak can be made stronger when exposed to this smoke.

Hōzōmon Gate

In the 1964 phase of reconstruction, the temple treasures were stored on the top of one of the gates. As a result that gate came to be known as the "Hōzō" gate; literally meaning "Treasury" gate.

Gojū-no-Tō or Five Story Pagoda

In Japan many of the large temples have three or five story roofed pagodas. In the case of the *Sensō-ji* temple, the five story pagoda, rebuilt in 1973 measures approximately 64 m in height.

The dragon is 14.5 m in length from head to tail

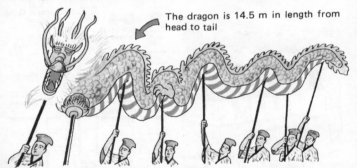

Kinryū-no-Mai or The Golden Dragon Dance (Held on March 18)

Legend has it that at the time the statue of *Kan-non*, enshrined in the *Sensō-ji* temple, first appeared a great golden dragon danced its way down to earth from the heavens. For this reason a Golden Dragon Dance is held every year. Since the dragon, weighs over 75 kg, it takes 8 strong young men to support it when performing the dance.

Nakamisé Shopping Street

Nakamisé Shopping Street is approximately a 300 m strip packed with small shops lining both sides of the street leading to the *Hōzōmon* Gate from the *Kaminarimon* Gate. The *Nakamisé* area has undergone steady constant growth since the initial stages of the Edo period, at the beginning of 17C.

There are many shops in the *Nakamisé* Shopping Street which sell objects that impress one with a feeling of being uniquely Japanese. The little shops offer a jam packed selection of all sorts of highly interesting souvenirs to take back home.

At present, when combined with its more recent outgrowth, the adjacent *Shin-Nakamisé* Shopping Street, the total number of shops comes to 150.

Welcome to the Wonderful World of Traditional Japanese Toys

Tako, or Kites

A wide variety of kites reminiscent of the Edo period are illustrated with the faces of actors, *Samurai* or elegant ladies from that era.

Rikishi Koma, or Toy Sumō Wrestlers

Place two figures of the *sumō* wrestlers in the center of a round tray. When the plate is deftly shaken in a light circular motion, the two *sumō* figures approach each other to begin to do battle. The first one to fall loses the match!

Také Tombo, or Bamboo Flyer

A piece of bamboo is whittled into the shape of a propeller blade with a round smooth stick attached in the center. To play, clasp the stick in the palm of both hands and rub your hands away from each other with a sudden forceful movement to spin the bamboo propeller. The circular motion will lift the toy up into the air and fly away!

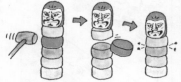

Daruma Otoshi, or The Knock Down Daruma

The pieces are knocked out one by one using a small wooden hammer. The object of the game is to knock out all of the torso pieces without toppling either the head of the *Daruma* or the entire torso itself.

Awashimadō Temple

On the west side of *Hondō*, or the Main Hall stands a small building dedicated to the guardian deity of women, otherwise known as *Awashima Myōjin*, or the Gracious God of *Awashima*.

It has been said that this benevolent and respected deity of *Awashima* has helped women by effectively treating and relieving all sorts of maladies and disorders particular to the fair sex.

A specially made large cake of *Tōfu*, or soybean curd, is stuck with all the old, dulled and broken needles.

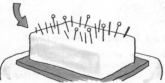

Hari-kuyō, or the Requiem Ceremony for Broken Needles (Held on February 8)

It is on this day that all forms of used, worn and broken sewing implements are put to their final rest. The ceremony is held every year on February 8 as an opportunity to pay one's last respects and express appreciation to all the sewing needles that had served well.

Dembōin Temple

Situated just this side on the left of the *Hōzōmon* Gate lies *Dembōin*, the site of the *Hombō*, or living quaters of the Buddhist priests. This structure erected in 1777 consists of various rooms among which are a kitchen, a reception hall for the use of respected visitors, an official entrance hall, and a *Shisha-no-ma*, or Special emissary room where messenger of the *Shōgun*, or Supreme Commander, were received.

The gate into Dembōin

Dembōin exudes an atmosphere of serenity where one can relax and commune with nature. Applications for admittance into this residence are possible if made in advance on an individual basis.

Five Story Pagoda

Ten'yū-an

Shinji Pond

Hombō (residence)

Main Gate

The Dembōin Gardens

The lovely gardens of *Dembōin* cover a surface area of 11,950 m². One can enjoy the beauty of form in this natural setting with the *Shinji* Pond serving as the central theme. A famous garden landscaper in the Edo period, named *Kobori Enshū*, was called on to design the garden.

TOKYO FAIRS

In Tokyo, much of the old folklore from the Edo period that the common people in the *Shitamachi* (Old Downtown area) have come to know and love is still preserved in modern times in the form of seasonal markets. A visit to any of these seasonal markets (*Ichi*) will provide you with an opportunity to enjoy some of the sights, sounds and traditions of the Edo period.

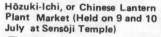

Hōzuki-Ichi, or Chinese Lantern Plant Market (Held on 9 and 10 July at Sensōji Temple)

The day upon which *Hōzuki*, or Chinese Lantern Plants are sold is known as the *Shiman-rokusen-nichi*, literally 46,000 Days. Since it is believed that those who purchase the Chinese Lantern Plants at the *Sensōji* Temple on this day will benefit from 46,000 days worth of good fortune.

Hagoita-Ichi, or Battledore and Shuttlecock Market (Held on 17, 18, 19 December at Sensōji Temple)

This is an annual market event held near the end of the year. The surface of the wooden battledore is exquisitely decorated with the form of a *Kabuki* actor or an elegant lady from the Edo period.

Ōji-Inari no Tako-Ichi, or the Ōji Inari Shrine Kite Market (Held in the beginning of February)

Since most Japanese houses in the old days were made exclusively out of wood, there were many fires. For this reason *Hibusé no Yakkodako* kites were given to individuals to promote the idea of fire prevention.

Hibusé no Yakkodako

Asagao-Ichi (Held on the 6,7,8 July at the Iriya Kishibojin Temple)

The *Asagao Ichi* (Morning Glory Market) has been flourishing since its establishment in the latter half of the Edo period (the beginning of 19C.)

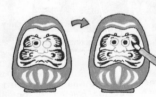

Daruma-Ichi, or Daruma Market (Held on 3,4 March at Jindaiji Temple)
Within the precincts of temples, shops display line upon line of large and small papier mâché *Daruma*s along their counters. It is the custom that when one has had the good fortune to gain a request wished for, one of the *Daruma's* eyes can be painted in.

27

● 浅草神社
ASAKUSA SHRINE

● Ginza Subway Line / 6 min. north of Asakusa Sta.

The *Asakusa* Shrine is dedicated to three men who were deified as a result of their involvement with the main object of worship at *Sensōji* Temple, the statue of *Kan-non*. Established to revere the memory of these three men, it is also called "*Sanja-sama*" or shrine of the three venerable ones. Every year in May, the *Sanja* Festival is held at the shrine.

The brilliant structure of the *Asakusa* Shrine is painted vermilion red accented with beautiful, multicolored wood carvings.

Construction of the shrine began in the initial stages of the Edo period in 1649.

Honden, or main sanctuary

Ishi-no-ma

Haiden, or outer hall

The *Asakusa* Shrine was designed such that the *Haiden,* or outer hall would be connected to the *Honden,* or main sanctuary by a room between the two called the *Ishi-no-ma*. This H-shaped structure style, *"Gongen zukuri"* was considered representative of Edo period shrine architecture.

At the entrance to the *Asakusa* Shrine, there is a stone *Torii*, or *Shintō* Shrine Archway.

A pair of *Komainu*, or stone dogs, face each other at the entrance to the compound. Considered to be mythical lions transformed into stone dogs, they serve as guardian deities of the shrine.

Senja-fuda, or Votive Card

In Japan, it is quite common to find small slips of paper known as *Senja-fuda* pasted in various locations within the precincts of a temple or shrine. The name, address and other such personal information about the worshipper are written on these slips.

When pasted on various structures, they demonstrate to others personal pride and devotion in visiting shrines or temples.

29

• 三社まつり
SANJA MATSURI

● **Held for four days starting on the third Sunday in May**

The *Sanja Matsuri* Festival held every year in May is the most popular event of the Asakusa Shrine. Over one hundred *Mikoshi* (portable shrines) march in procession through the streets of the Asakusa district. Various other traditional forms of entertainment are also performed for the public. The *Sanja Matsuri* Festival is noted as one of the big three Tokyo festivals.

The highlight of the *Sanja Matsuri* festival is the fanfare surrounding the *Miya-Dashi* and *Miya-iri* events.

Hachimaki, or twisted head band

Hanten, or a short coat

Zōri, or Japanese sandals

The local people wear a particularly distinctive style of clothing when parading the portable shrine through the streets. A Chinese symbol emblazoned on the back of the *Hanten* serves as an emblem of the local *Mikoshi* group to which the participant belongs.

Tekomai

The *Tekomai* is the one occasion when *Geisha* don men's clothing and lead the *Mikoshi* procession with their own particular form of dance. This *Geisha* pageant originating in the Edo period, adds a colorful note to the contemporary *Mikoshi* processions.

Binzasara-mai

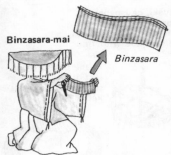

Binzasara

A rather unusual dance is performed in the *Sanja Matsuri* Festival using a traditional percussion instrument called a *Binzasara*. It consists of 108 thin wooden slats attached together by a string passing through them. It is stretched and contracted to produce its unique sounds.

Shishimai

The *Shishimai*, or Mythical Lion Mask Dance, is also performed along with the *Binzasara* dance. A costume of this lion has been worn by dancers since long ago in order to drive off evil spirits.

EDO STYLE CUISINE [1]

Ever since long ago, people in Tokyo have been able to choose from a wide selection of traditional confectionary delights to satisfy their cravings for sweets. These various local specialities are also taken along as small souvenirs when going on visits to other parts of the country.

Kaminari Okoshi, or Thunder Brittle

This hard, brittle-like candy is made by mixing puffed rice or wheat with sugar syrup.

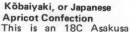

Kōbaiyaki, or Japanese Apricot Confection

This is an 18C Asakusa speciality made with flour and sugar.

In the past this confection was sold in small bamboo baskets.

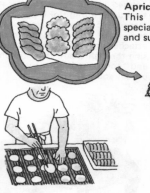

Superior quality rice crackers are baked by an expert confectioner.

Sanshoku Sembei, or Three Color Rice Crackers

Three different types of rice crackers are made using white sugar, brown soy sauce and green tea to give the crackers both their taste and coloring.

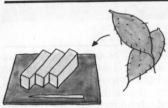

Nuré Amanattō Beans
This is a confection made from a large grain variety of the *azuki* bean. The beans are soft, sweet and delicious. A well-known Tokyo delicacy.

Imoyōkan, or Sweet Potato Jelly
This is a variation of the usual *yōkan,* or sweet bean jelly, using sweet potato as the main ingredient rather than *azuki* beans.

Kuzumochi cakes
Kuzumochi cakes are made from arrow root flour mixed with water then kneaded into round little cakes. They are eaten with light molasses and soybean powder as a topping. A *Kameido Tenjin* shrine treat since 1805.

The shape of this candy is made using scissors.

Eitarō Candy
This candy has been made from an old traditional recipe since the end of the Edo period (19C).

Reasonably priced, it is well loved by the common people.

• 隅田川

SUMIDA RIVER

Ever since the Edo period, the big river called *Sumidagawa* has played an important role in the lives of the common people. The Sumida River cuts right through the commercial heart of Tokyo. It has been said that although it has undergone tremendous technological development, the Sumida River still retains many different aspects of Edo culture. At present a total of 27 public and private transportation bridges (including railroads) span the Sumida River.

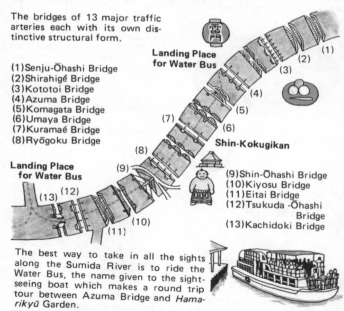

The bridges of 13 major traffic arteries each with its own distinctive structural form.

(1) Senju-Ōhashi Bridge
(2) Shirahige Bridge
(3) Kototoi Bridge
(4) Azuma Bridge
(5) Komagata Bridge
(6) Umaya Bridge
(7) Kuramae Bridge
(8) Ryōgoku Bridge

Landing Place for Water Bus

Shin-Kokugikan

Landing Place for Water Bus

(9) Shin-Ōhashi Bridge
(10) Kiyosu Bridge
(11) Eitai Bridge
(12) Tsukuda -Ōhashi Bridge
(13) Kachidoki Bridge

The best way to take in all the sights along the Sumida River is to ride the Water Bus, the name given to the sightseeing boat which makes a round trip tour between Azuma Bridge and *Hamarikyū* Garden.

The Sumidagawa Fireworks Display
The fireworks display was celebrated as one of those events that lended charm to the summer season. The Sumida River Fireworks Display is a highly popular event with a long history dating back 250 years. The event draws large numbers of people to witness this brilliant evening spectacle.

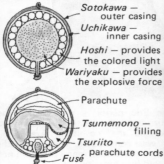

Yakata-bune
The interior of the *Yakata-bune,* or Japanese style houseboat, is designed so that one may eat and drink seated on *tatami* mat while enjoying the outdoor scenery.

Hanabi, or Fireworks

The techniques used in making fireworks were introduced to Japan in the 16th century. Japanese Fireworks are particularly noted for the development of the *Waridama*, rockets which produce spectacular starbursts to represent the forms of cherry blossoms, plum blossoms wysteria and various other flowers.

Sotokawa — outer casing
Uchikawa — inner casing
Hoshi — provides the colored light
Wariyaku — provides the explosive force
Parachute
Tsumemono — filling
Tsuriito — parachute cords
Fusé

Midori-Yanagi   *Ao-Botan*   *Yanagi*

350
300
250
200
150
100
50
m

· 吉原

YOSHIWARA

Yoshiwara, the licensed prostitution district, was a highly prosperous area from 1657 to 1957. At the height of its notoriety in the Edo period there were more than 3,000 prostitutes referred to as courtesans. The area was bustling with the constant movement of men in search of sexual favors. In contrast, the present Yoshiwara area has become a cosy, respectable amusement center.

Tayū, or Top-Rank Courtesans
Courtesan who attained the highest rank in their profession were called *Tayū*. They are equally endowed with both intelligence as well as beauty.

In the case of the *Tayū*, a huge *Obi* was knotted in the front.

The *Tayū* were garbed in elegant costumes. These costumes often weighed as much as 20 kg.

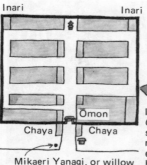

Inari   Inari

Ōmon

Chaya   Chaya

Mikaeri Yanagi, or willow

In the Edo period a moat called the *Ohaguro-dobu*, or the tooth black moat, surrounded the Yoshiwara Area. This moat was constructed to prevent the escape of courtesans, many of whom had been sold into prostitution.

Tayū Courtesan Performances

In the shadowy world of the courtesan, there was a strict protocol observed in the dealings between the clients and the *Tayū* courtesans. Many of these practices are recreated in performances held during dinner shows at the present day Yoshiwara.

Restaurants in the licensed quarters called *Hikité-chaya* served as an intermediary to guide the clients to the rooms of the courtesans.

Kamuro —
a little girl attendant

A *Tayū* was accompanied on her promenades by *Kamuro* and *Furisodé-Shinzō*.

A pledge is made in the exchange of cups of *saké*. Accepting the filled cup in both hands, the client sips the *saké* three times.

A *Tayū* dance is also performed.

In turn the *Tayū* takes the cup in one hand and takes three sips.

TOKYO FOLK CRAFTS

Edo City was a thriving center of Japanese culture in the Edo period. Many fine craftsmen gathered in this town to practice their trade. The unusual crafts that they produced as well as the techniques used to make them have been passed on to the present. They have become the noted products of the Tokyo area.

Chiyogami paper is printed using a carved wood block upon which coloring is applied.

Edo Chiyogami Paper
Chiyogami refers to the pattern printed on small sized *washi,* or Japanese paper. Various aspects and customs of the society at that time were reflected in the many unique patterns of the *Edo chiyogami* paper.

Kumihimo Cord
Kumihimo cord uses an assortment of colored threads woven together to create this particular type of craft.

Uchiwa Fan
It was considered quite fashionable to go for a stroll carrying a *uchiwa* fan with some pattern matching one's particular mood of the day.

Oshié Battledore

Oshié is a relief art type of ornamentation created by stuffing the inside of the cut cloth form of a sketch with cotton thus resulting in the protruding outline of the design. This technique was used to decorate the battledores.

The basic design is sketched on the cloth.

Each individual part is filled in with color.

The finished product.

Heated glass is stuck to the end of a special pipe. Blowing through the pipe expands the glass form into a thin ball used to make the windbell.

Edo Fūrin Windbells

Edo Fūrin Windbells made out of glass are sold at the Chinese Lantern Plant Market. (see p. 26)

Tsumami Kanzashi Hairpins

Tsumami Kanzashi hairpins are decorated with tiny pieces of cloth made to appear like flowers.

Edo Chōchin, or Paper Lanterns

"*Edo Moji*", stylized characters of the Japanese writing system are painted on these paper lanterns.

UENO

Originally, Ueno was a temple town adjacent to the *Kan-eiji* Temple. This town came to be known by the common people for its cogenial atmosphere. Ueno station was built after the start of the Meiji period (1883) as the departure point for trains heading north to the *Tōhoku* region.

Ueno Park is the site of various historical spots. Among these are the numerous art and science museums, a zoo and the *Kan-eiji* Temple. The shopping area is definitely a place worth visiting.

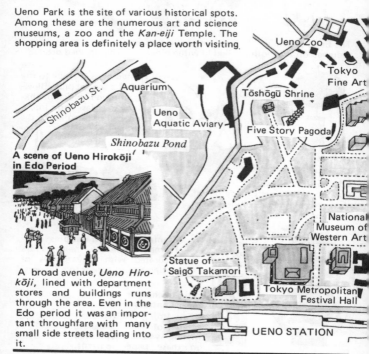

Shinobazu St.

Aquarium

Ueno Zoo

Tokyo Fine Art

Tōshōgū Shrine

Ueno Aquatic Aviary

Five Story Pagoda

Shinobazu Pond

A scene of Ueno Hirokōji in Edo Period

A broad avenue, *Ueno Hirokōji*, lined with department stores and buildings runs through the area. Even in the Edo period it was an important throughfare with many small side streets leading into it.

Statue of Saigō Takamori

National Museum of Western Art

Tokyo Metropolitan Festival Hall

UENO STATION

40

Amé Yoko Street

The street adjacent to Ueno station is called *Amé Yoko* Street. An abundant selection of reasonably priced goods are available there. This area is always swarming with people looking for bargains.

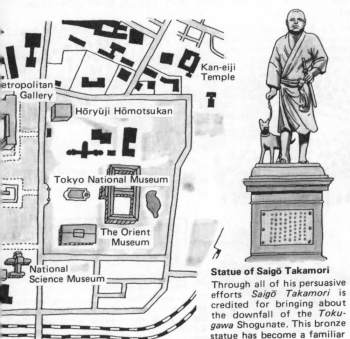

Kan-eiji Temple

etropolitan Gallery

Hōryūji Hōmotsukan

Tokyo National Museum

The Orient Museum

National Science Museum

Statue of Saigō Takamori

Through all of his persuasive efforts *Saigō Takamori* is credited for bringing about the downfall of the *Tokugawa* Shogunate. This bronze statue has become a familiar Ueno landmark.

● 寛永寺

KAN-EIJI TEMPLE

● JR   Yamanoté Line / 7 min. west of Uguisudani Sta.

The *Kan-eiji* Temple was established in 1625 by the Buddhist high priest, *Tenkai*, who performed the purification rites to protect Edo Castle from the ravages of fire. In the Edo period, the temple covered an immense surface area of 1,188,000 m². *Kiyomizudō* Hall and a five story pagoda serve as reminders of its past glory.

In the Edo period, 36 temple buildings and 36 ancillary buildings were centered around the original main temple structure.

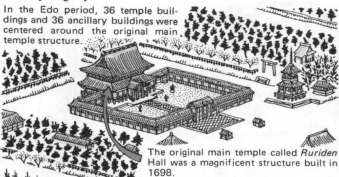

The original main temple called *Ruriden* Hall was a magnificent structure built in 1698.

The present main temple was brought to the site from the *Kawagoé Kitain* Temple in 1879. An Imperial scroll with the Emperor's personal autograph from the former *Ruriden* Temple is hanging in this main Hall.

Kiyomizudō Temple

Kiyomizu Temple in Kyoto

This hall was patterned after the *Kiyomizu* Temple located in Kyoto. Most unusual is the construction of a exact replica of its stage.

Jizō, The Icon Oracle of Jōmeiin

Jōmeiin is one of the ancillary temples of the Kan-eiji Temple. People invoke this stone image of *Jizō* to foretell their chances of being granted a divine wish. It is believed that if one is easily able to raise the 30 cm high statue, they are assured of good luck.

Habutaé Dango

Habutaé Dango Dumplings have been a familiar confectionary delight to people in the Ueno neighborhood since the Edo period. These particular dumplings are velvety in consistency and as smooth to the palate as *Habutaé* silk is to the touch.

43

TŌSHŌGŪ SHRINE

• JR   Yamanoté Line / 8 min. northwest of Ueno Sta.

The *Tōshōgū* Shrine is dedicated to the first generation founder of the *Tokugawa* Shogunate, *Tokugawa Ieyasu*. This shrine was established in 1627. The existing structure was re-modeled in 1651 by the third generation *Shōgun*, *Tokugawa Iemitsu*.

The main shrine building, *Konjiki-den*, or The Golden Hall is a magnificent, ornate building. At the beginning of the Edo period it was luxuriously decorated with glittering furnishings.

The *Haiden,* or Outer Hall, is furnished with murals painted by famed Edo period artist, *Kanō Tan-yū*.

Karamon Gate
The arched Chinese style gate is decorated with dragons ascending and descending to and from Heaven. Legend has it that when night falls, these dragons go to the *Shinobazu* Pond to drink their fill.

The Ueno Flower Viewing Season

Ever since olden times people in Japan have enjoyed watching cherry blossoms while drinking *saké*. This is known as *Hanami*, or Flower viewing. Ueno is one of the more noted locations teeming with hordes of people who come every year to take in the cherry blossoms.

Ueno park has approximately 1,000 cherry trees. At its peak the main promenade, a veritable archway of cherry blossoms, becomes a truly lovely sight. Evening flower viewing is fantastic.

Hanami flower viewing parties are often held on a mat spread out under a cherry tree.

Even in the Edo period scores of people would visit Ueno to see the cherry blossoms.

• 不忍池

SHINOBAZU POND

● JR Yamanoté Line / 5 min. west of Ueno Sta.

Shinobazu Pond is located in the southwest corner of Ueno Park. The 2 km circumference of this huge pond was ringed with many popular eating spots during the Edo period. People would come together on a warm summer night to dance the traditional *"Bon-odori"* and partake of *saké* in this area. *(Edo-shumi Nōryō Taikai)*

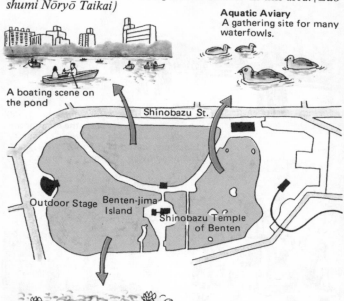

Aquatic Aviary
A gathering site for many waterfowls.

A boating scene on the pond

Shinobazu St.

Outdoor Stage

Benten-jima Island

Shinobazu Temple of Benten

In the summer the surface of Shinobazu Pond is resplendent with the appearance of many lotus blossoms.

The Shinobazu Temple of Benten

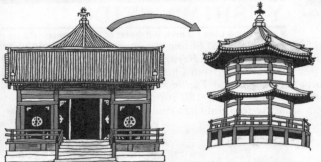

A small island in the center of the pond is the site of the Goddess of Fortune.

The Temple of *Benten* was originally built in the first half of 16C. Reconstruction of the present version was completed in 1958.

Biwa, lute

In front of the Temple stands a statue of the four stringed lute of *Benzaiten (Benten)*.

Benzaiten (Benten)
Originally *Benzaiten* was venerated as the Goddess of the River. Following this, she became the guardian deity of wisdom, the pursuit of knowledge and the arts. Finally she was acknowledged as the Goddess of Money.

● 湯島聖堂

YUSHIMA SEIDŌ

● JR Chūō Line / 3 min. northeast of Ochanomizu Sta.

In 1603 *Yushima Seidō* Shrine was constructed at *Shinobu-ga-oka* in the Ueno area by *Hayashi Razan*. The shrine dedicated to this Ancient Sage from China was moved to Yushima and appropriately renamed *Yushima Seidō* Shrine in the year 1690. In the latter half of the 18C it became *Shōheizaka Gakumon-jo*, an academy for Confucian studies.

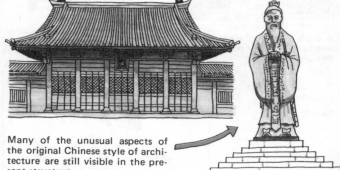

Many of the unusual aspects of the original Chinese style of architecture are still visible in the present structure.

Hayashi Razan (1583—1657)
Confucius scholar at the beginning of the Edo period.

Shōheizaka Academy in Edo period

VARIETY THEATERS

The Ueno district has been considered a lively center of social activity among the common people since the Edo times. Many popular performances were held there. Today a considerable number of the performance halls still remain and provide various forms of traditional entertainment to countless numbers of theater goers.

Suzumoto Engeijō

This is the oldest variety theater in all of Tokyo where *Rakugo* and *Kōdan*, or Story telling (See next page) are performed.

wooden exchange ticket

Since the interior is furnished with *tatami* mats, theater goers are required to remove their shoes and sit on floor cushions.

RAKUGO · KŌDAN

Rakugo and *Kōdan* are two of the many forms of entertainment that the common people have enjoyed since the Edo period. They are performed mainly in a *Yosé* Hall which is somewhat similar to a western-style variety theater.

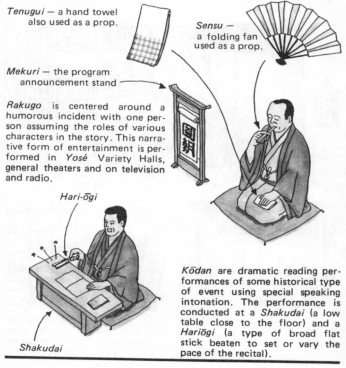

Tenugui — a hand towel also used as a prop.

Sensu — a folding fan used as a prop.

Mekuri — the program announcement stand

Rakugo is centered around a humorous incident with one person assuming the roles of various characters in the story. This narrative form of entertainment is performed in *Yosé* Variety Halls, general theaters and on television and radio.

Hari-ōgi

Shakudai

Kōdan are dramatic reading performances of some historical type of event using special speaking intonation. The performance is conducted at a *Shakudai* (a low table close to the floor) and a *Hariōgi* (a type of broad flat stick beaten to set or vary the pace of the recital).

Success in the world of *Rakugo* and *Kōdan* can only be achieved by rising through the apprenticeship system. Both the stage name and the functions of the *Rakugo* or *Kōdan* master are passed on from generation to generation through this system.

Former illustrious figures in the more recent history of *Rakugo* had enjoyed continuous popularity throughout their careers.

The fifth generation Kokontei Shinshō. Ad lib being his forté, he was highly rated among *Rakugo* artists for his unrestrained natural style of performance.

The sixth generation San-yūtei Enshō. Known for the great importance that he placed on the basics of the art form, he led an influential school of *Rakugo* with a wide repetoire of performances.

The eighth generation Katsura Bunraku. Endless rehearsals resulted in flawless performances which attracted large audiences wishing to see this accomplished *Rakugo* artist.

● 下町風俗資料館

SHITAMACHI FOLK MUSEUM

● **JR Yamanoté Line / 2 min. south of Ueno Sta.**

Shitamachi is the old, traditional district where merchants, craftsmen and other common people settled (see p.11). It is established in 1980 to attempt to hold back the relentless march of time and to preserve customs and fashions of the old *Shitamachi* district that are on the verge of total extinction.

All the objects on display in the museum were donated by people presently living in the *Shitamachi* district. Only in this way one can really witness first hand the customs, fashions and way of life in *Shitamachi*.

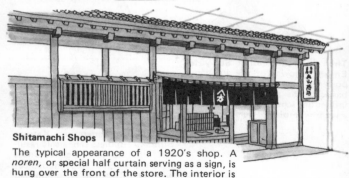

Shitamachi Shops

The typical appearance of a 1920's shop. A *noren,* or special half curtain serving as a sign, is hung over the front of the store. The interior is divided into rooms with dirt floors or *tatami* mats.

A particularly distinctive characteristic most often associated with the typical *Shitamachi* character is the great importance placed on being dapper in both fashion and manner.

Ramuné is a popular carbonated beverage that *Shitamachi* children loved to drink.

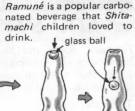

glass ball

Just punch down the glass ball (that holds in the fizz) and you're ready for an old time treat.

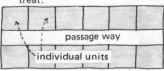

passage way

individual units

In the *Shitamachi* district *Nagaya*, long and narrow shaped structures partitioned into separate dwellings were clustered into certain areas to form neighborhoods of tenement row houses.

Tōfu sale

Red pepper sale

Goods Popular in the Shitamachi district
Although previously all sorts of goods were sold in the *Shitamachi* district, it is almost impossible to find them in shops today.

Tempura, Soba and *Sushi* are all equally representative of Japanese style cooking. These are some of the more familiar dishes that the common people since the Edo period have come to know and love.

Tempura

A dish made from fish and vegetables dipped in a light batter then deep fried.

Fixed menu meals can be ordered in a *Tempura* restaurant. The meal set consists of various kinds of *tempura* accompanied with white rice, *miso* soup, and Japanese style pickled vegetables.

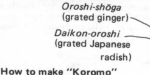

Oroshi-shōga
(grated ginger)

Daikon-oroshi
(grated Japanese radish)

Tempura is eaten dipped in a soy sauce broth.

How to make "Koromo"

Ice water

1) Sift flour in a bowl
2) Mix eggs with water.
3) The egg and water mixture is then lightly beat in with the flour.

54

Soba, or Buckwheat Noodles

Soba are long, thin noodles made from buckwheat flour. *Soba* are eaten either cold in the *Mori soba*-style or hot in a soy sauce based soup.

Yutō

Tokkuri(flask) containing *taré* (soy based broth)

Dish for broth

After all is eaten, patrons usually add *Sobayu,* the hot water used to boil noodles to the remaining soy broth and drink it as a tasty soup supplement to the meal.

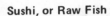

Kitsuné Soba
Deep fried *tōfu* (boiled with sugar and soy sauce) is placed on top of the noodles.

Tsukimi Soba
A raw egg is placed on top of the buckwheat noodles.

Sushi, or Raw Fish

Vinegared rice is rolled into small oval balls and topped with various kinds of fresh fish and shell fish.

Neta (topping)

sushi rice

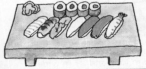

The most important qualities of any good *sushi* shop must be the freshness of its fish and the friendly, animated attitude of its chefs.

NIHOMBASHI

Nihombashi Bridge was built in 1603 as one important part of the infrastructure of Edo town. It has also become the fixed point for the measurement of distance for the Japanese road system. This area flourished as the metropolitan center of the capital. Many people would come to do business in the many shops lining the streets leading to Nihombashi Bridge.

"Nihombashi" (the name currently posted on the bridge) was written by the 15th generation *Shōgun, Tokugawa Yoshinobu.*

日本橋

The 0 mile Marker

A copper plaque was laid in the center of the bridge as the fixed marker point for measuring distance in the Japanese road system.

The current bridge was built in 1911. It is a Renaissance style structure 49 m long and 27 m wide.

Under this famous bridge flows the Nihombashi River. This was a major water transportation route during the Edo period.

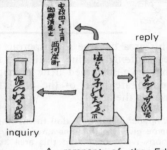

reply

inquiry

A remnent of the Edo period, the "Lost Child" stone still stands at Nihombashi Bridge. At its time this stone served as message board for missing children.

Toki-no-Kané (Nihombashi Kokuchō)

Cast in 1711. This bell which sounded the passing of the hours to the town people of the Edo period lies preserved in the Nihombashi Bridge.

Based on a lunar calendar, the 12 horary signs were used for marking the passage of time.

• 人形町

NINGYŌCHŌ

This area became a prosperous town near the frequently visited *Suitengū* Shrine, dedicated to the god of childbirth. Since the town sustained little damage during World War ll, many people are fond of the old Edo downtown charm that surrounds the area.

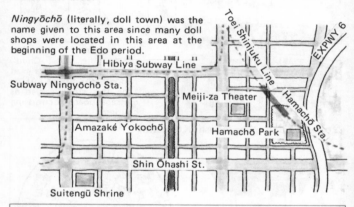

Ningyōchō (literally, doll town) was the name given to this area since many doll shops were located in this area at the beginning of the Edo period.

Toei Shinjuku Line

EXPWY 6

Hibiya Subway Line

Subway Ningyōchō Sta.

Meiji-za Theater

Hamachō Sta.

Amazaké Yokochō

Hamachō Park

Shin Ōhashi St.

Suitengū Shrine

Ningyō-yaki Confection

Ningyō-yaki are soft, baked confection shaped in a variety of popular doll forms.

An — sweet bean paste

The unusual shapes of the *Ningyō-yaki* Confection are made by baking wheat flour batter poured into a mold with sweet bean paste in the center.

Suitengū Shrine

The *Suitengū* Shrine is a well-known shrine sacred to the God of Easy Delivery and Safe Childbirth. Many women have called upon this deity for a safe outcome to their pregnancy.

Inu-Hariko

The *Suitengū* Shrine sells papier mache dogs. These mascots symbolize the hope of being accorded divine favour for an easy delivery.

Five Chinese characters forming a charm are written on a piece of paper. They are then torn off and drunk in a predetermined order as a means of avoiding misfortune from a complicated delivery.

The bell at the front of the *Suitengū* Shrine is attached to a rope made from a red and white cloth. This cloth is often used as a belly band with which women gird the abdomen to insure safe and easy childbirth.

In the neighborhood adjacent to *Suitengū* Shrine, confection shaped in the form of charms are sold.

59

• 向島

MUKŌJIMA

In the northwest part of *Sumida* Ward along the *Sumida* river lies an area known as *Mukōjima*. The nearby embankment is a noted site for cherry blossoms. Also a celebrated site for viewing the moon, this site was a favorite resort of the Edo towns' people. At present this site near *Kototoi* Bridge has become *Sumida Park*.

Mukōjima Hyakkaen Flower Garden

Meeting place

Rest spot

This garden was established in 1804. Plants mentioned in old Japanese and Chinese literary classics were gathered in the roughly 10,000 m² surface area of the park.

The flower archway of Japanese bush clover (*Hagi*) is particularly lovely.

Kototoi Dango Dumplings

There is a shop near the Kototoi Bridge which sells dumplings with the name of the bridge.

Ushijima Jinja Shrine

Built in 860, a bronze statue of a cow, *Nadéushi,* stands in front of the main sanctuary of the shrine. It is believed that those who stroke the part of the cow corresponding to that part of their own body ailing will be cured.

The Sakura Mochi Rice cakes of Chōmeiji Temple

Rice cake filled with sweet bean paste is wrapped in a salt cured aromatic cherry tree leaf.

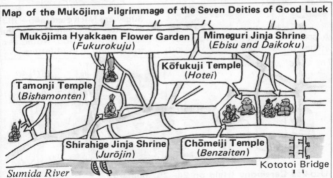

Map of the Mukōjima Pilgrimmage of the Seven Deities of Good Luck

Mukōjima Hyakkaen Flower Garden (*Fukurokuju*)

Mimeguri Jinja Shrine (*Ebisu and Daikoku*)

Kōfukuji Temple (*Hotei*)

Tamonji Temple (*Bishamonten*)

Shirahige Jinja Shrine (*Jurōjin*)

Chōmeiji Temple (*Benzaiten*)

Sumida River

Kototoi Bridge

The Pilgrimmage of the Seven Deities of Good Luck (Shichifukujin)

In Japan there is a belief that those who visit certain temples and shrines venerating a select group of seven deities (*Shichifukujin*) will be granted good fortune.

● 亀戸天神

KAMEIDO TENJIN

● JR Sōbu Line/10 min. north of Kameido Sta.

This is the shrine where the deified spirit of 9 C scholar *Sugawara Michizané* is venerated. He is known to all as a deity of study and learning. The *Kameido Tenjin* Shrine built in 1663 was modeled after the *Dazaifu Temmangū* Shrine in Kyūshū. This shrine is always frequented by those praying for success on school entrance examinations.

A scene of Wisteria blossoms by an arched bridge from the Edo period.

Sugawara Michizané(845—903) Minister of State from the early Heian period. Noted as a scholar and man of letters.

The "*Uso*"wood carving

Uso-kaé Ceremony (Held on 24—25, January)

This event of the new year has been held ever since 1820. Old wood carvings of a bullfinch (*Uso* in Japanese) are exchanged for new ones. The new carvings of these birds which people try to receive are considered to summon forth good luck.

● 両国

RYŌGOKU

In the early stages of the Edo period the town that developed around *Ryōgoku* Bridge flourished as a center of commercial activity. Presently the area is a well-known *Sumō* (see next page) town centered around *Shin-kokugikan* Stadium.

The Landscape of Ryōgokubashi in Edo period

The Shin-kokugikan Stadium

This ground hall is where *Sumō* Wrestling, the true Japanese national sport is held. The newly built structure was completed in 1983.

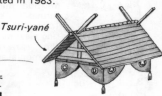

Tsuri-yané

Tokudawara

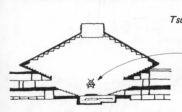

Inside in the center of the Stadium lies a raised dirt mound, the *Dohyō*, or *Sumō* ring. The *Dohyō* can be stored away when not in use thus making the stadium available for other events.

Dohyō — *Sumō* ring

63

相撲

SUMŌ

Sumō is a unique style of traditional wrestling which is distinctively Japanese. It has drawn its support from countless generations who have enjoyed watching this time-honored national past time. Grand *Sumō* Tournaments are held six times a year. The *Shin-kokugikan* Stadium in Tokyo hosts three of those events.

The gargantuan *Rikishi*, or *Sumō* Wrestler must have agility to match his power in order to outmaneuver an opponent.

magé — topknot

Gumbai

Gyōji — referee

Keshō-mawashi

A *Sumō* wrestler ranked in the top position makes his formal entrance (*Dohyō-iri*) into the ring wearing the *Ke-shō mawashi*, or ceremonial apron.

mawashi — belt

Sagari — apron

Shiko

Sonkyo

Shikiri

Kanjinzumō

In the Edo period *Kanjinzumō* events were held to collect funds for the construction of shrines, temples and bridges. These events became so popular that such amateur events gradually led to the foundation of *Sumō* Wrestling as a professional sport.

Basic Rules

Two wrestlers are pitted against each other in the ring. The first to go out of the ring or to be brought to the ground loses the match.

| **Tsukidashi** | **Uwatenagé** | **Yorikiri** |

Chanko-nabé Cooking

Chanko-nabé is a well known type of pot cooking popular among *Sumō* wrestlers. There are a number of restaurants specializing in this *Sumō* dish in the *Ryōgoku* area.

chicken
vegetables
fish
tōfu

KATSUSHIKA

In the Edo period water flowing in from various rivers served to make Katsushika a great zone for rice paddies. The present area has been almost completely converted for residential and industrial use. However, there still are an abundant number of parks for water craft, fishery experimentation stations and various other river facilities.

There are a considerable number of sites where a number of highly interesting historical events took place.

Mizumoto Park

This is a rather unusual riverside district park within the metropolitan Tokyo area.

Shibararé Jizō

This statue of *Jizō* would be tied with a rope when praying for a certain wish.

Yagiri-no-Watashi, or Yagiri Ferry Crossing

In all of Tokyo this is the only remaining site where people can be ferried across the river in Japanese style row boats just as they were in ages past.

Shibamata Taishakuten Temple

The formal name of this temple built in 1629 is *Daikyōji* Temple. However, since the main object of worship is the Buddhist guardian deity, *Taishakuten*, it has often been called by this name. Numbers of people have been quite familiar with this temple as a place to seek relief from their ailments and to ward off evil influences.

The town of *Shibamata* itself is also quite well-known as the setting of the most popular movie series in all of Japan about a modern day folk hero called *Tora-san*, the Vagabond.

Within the temple compound stands a statue of a Buddhist saint considered capable of curing ailments. A straw brush to scrub the corresponding part of the statue would bring about relief from one's suffering.

Hajikisaru, or
The Jumping Monkey

This toy monkey is also considered a charm to ward off evil spirits. The toy has been sold at the *Taishakuten* Temple since the Edo period.

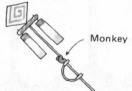

Monkey

出初め式
DEZOMÉ-SHIKI

● Held on 6 January at Harumi 5-chōmé

It was originally a fire drill ceremony held by local brigades at the beginning of the New Year. At present, the Tokyo Fire Fighter's parade is a Metropolitan Fire Department event consisting of drills and a fire engine parade. The highlight of the event, however, is the demonstration of traditional Edo period Fire Brigade techniques.

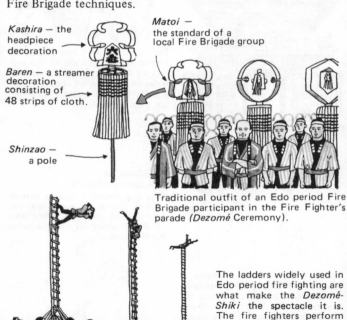

Kashira — the headpiece decoration

Baren — a streamer decoration consisting of 48 strips of cloth.

Shinzao — a pole

Matoi — the standard of a local Fire Brigade group

Traditional outfit of an Edo period Fire Brigade participant in the Fire Fighter's parade *(Dezomé* Ceremony).

The ladders widely used in Edo period fire fighting are what make the *Dezomé-Shiki* the spectacle it is. The fire fighters perform all sorts of acrobatic stunts on these ladders.

Machi-Hikeshi, or The Fire Fighters in Edo Period

In Edo, the former name of Tokyo, the general fire fighter structure consisted of groups of smaller fire brigades organized at the block level.

The members of the Fire Brigade were greatly admired as local heroes.

Water supplies were stored in various places throughout the local area for use in fire fighting.

Oké (pails)

Taru (barrel) filled with water

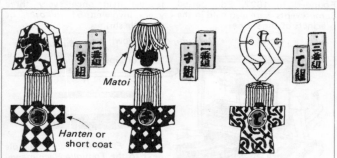

Matoi

Hanten or short coat

The Standard of a Local Fire Brigade Group

The personal insignia of the local group was affixed to all their short coats and standards.

● 深川

FUKAGAWA

This area was a thriving commercial district during the Edo period with streets lined with *Ryōtei* restaurants and tea houses. Highly animated festivals and many wholesale lumber shops each with their own timberyards reveal another aspect of this old Edo downtown area.

Tomioka Hachimangū Shrine
Founded in 1627, Edo period *Sumō* events were also held in the precincts of the shrine.

An extremely popular event is the festival held once every three years involving 51 *mikoshi*, or portable shrines.

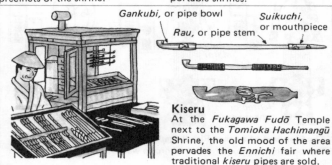

Gankubi, or pipe bowl

Rau, or pipe stem

Suikuchi, or mouthpiece

Kiseru
At the *Fukagawa Fudō* Temple next to the *Tomioka Hachimangū* Shrine, the old mood of the area pervades the *Ennichi* fair where traditional *kiseru* pipes are sold.

Traditional Fukagawa Attractions

Fukagawa was noted for the lively and spirited character of it's Edo period towns' people.

When handling the floating logs, *kawanami,* a log rolling technique is demonstrated as an acrobatic attraction.

Kakunori, or The Timberyard Log Rolling Event
(Held in October during the Grand Tokyo Festival.)

Logs floating on the water served as the actual spot for the timberyards. The present day site of log storage is in Tokyo Bay.

60 kg. (132 lbs.)
Kome-Dawara —
A straw rice bag

Sagachō Power Contest
(Held on the first Sunday in October.)

A acrobatic power contest retained from the Edo period is performed in Fukagawa.

TSUKIJI・TSUKUDAJIMA

This area was established from reclaimed land in the Tokyo Bay at the start of the Edo period (early 16 C). The present day Tsukiji is lined with street upon street of buildings and business offices. Tsukudajima, on the other hand, still bears a resemblance to the kind of area that existed there in the Edo period.

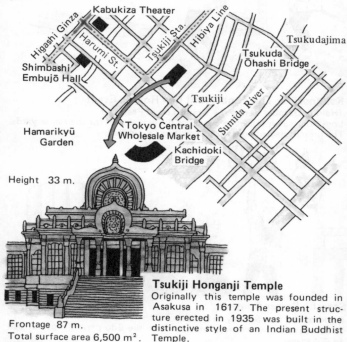

Height 33 m.

Frontage 87 m.
Total surface area 6,500 m².

Tsukiji Honganji Temple
Originally this temple was founded in Asakusa in 1617. The present structure erected in 1935 was built in the distinctive style of an Indian Buddhist Temple.

The Tokyo Central Wholesale Market

A market for the wholesale purchase of fresh produce, it is also known as the Tsukiji Fish Market. It was moved to the present site from the fish market located in Nihombashi. It's a spacious market place with a total surface area encompassing 210,000 m².

Tsukiji does a brisk business with fish shop owners and Japanese-style restaurant cooks who gather there from the very early hours of the morning.

Tsukudajima

A fisherman's village built in the Edo period, it currently has a large number of the 1920 houses standing in the area.

Sumiyoshi Jinja Shrine

This shrine was built for the fishing people in 1646. Once every three years a grand festival is held at which time unusual octagonal portable shrines are paraded about.

Tsukuda-ni Cooking

Tsukuda-ni is a precooked food which originally was intended for long term storage during deep sea voyages.

73

日本庭園
JAPANESE GARDENS

In the Edo period feudal lords called *Daimyōs* vaunted their wealth and power by creating elaborate, beautiful, natural setting gardens. In Tokyo, the following two represent the splendour of the gardens of former *Daimyōs*.

An Edo period book of garden landscaping, this book offers instruction in the proper way to lay out mountains, rivers, ponds and bridges in a harmonious fashion.

The route of this walking course winds its way across rivers and over bridges through various models of well-known Japanese settings.

Koishikawa Kōrakuen Garden
This garden was designed in 1629 by the *Mito* feudal clan. This garden has been designed with miniature lake and hills in the *Tsukiyama* style.

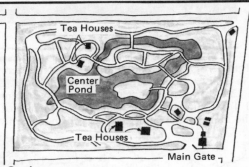

Rikugien Garden

Yanagisawa Yoshiyasu was a notable *Daimyō* who served as a highly capable aide to the *Shōgun*. In 1695 he took it upon himself to have a *Tsukiyama* style hill and lake garden built with a path meandering through various types of landscape scenery. The garden measures about 86,517 m².

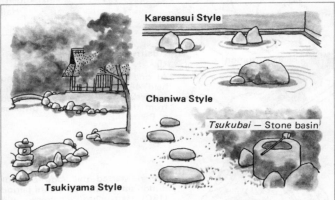

There are three types of Japanese gardens: the *Tsukiyama* nature in miniature, the *Karesansui* rock forms and the *Chaniwa* tea ceremony garden.

ZŌJŌJI TEMPLE

● **JR Yamanoté Line/10 min. west of Hamamatsuchō Sta.**

Zōjōji Temple of the *Jōdo* Buddhist sect, is the second largest temple in Tokyo after the *Ueno Kan-eiji* Temple. Originally built in 1393, the structure was moved to its present location in 1590. It grew in importance under the influence of the *Shōgun* to be the patron temple of the *Tokugawa* Family.

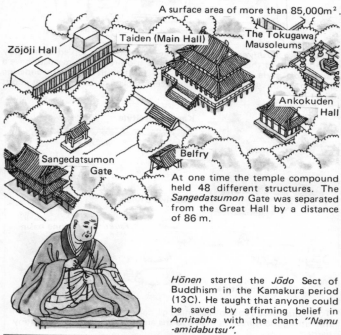

A surface area of more than 85,000m².

Zōjōji Hall

Taiden (Main Hall)

The Tokugawa Mausoleums

Ankokuden Hall

Sangedatsumon Gate

Belfry

At one time the temple compound held 48 different structures. The *Sangedatsumon* Gate was separated from the Great Hall by a distance of 86 m.

Hōnen started the *Jōdo* Sect of Buddhism in the Kamakura period (13C). He taught that anyone could be saved by affirming belief in *Amitabha* with the chant *"Namu-amidabutsu"*.

Height 21 m.

Front Surface 21 m.

Three statues of Gautama who attained Buddahood are installed in the second floor of the *Sangedatsumon* Gate.

The Sangedatsumon Gate

This is the main gate of the *Zōjōji* Temple, erected in 1605. This great two story tower gate was built in the Chinese style of that period.

The major portion of the mausoleum structure was completely destroyed.

Above the tomb of the 6th generation *Shōgun, Tokugawa Ienobu,* stands a bronze Treasure Tower. A stone room containing his tomb lies underground.

The Tokugawa Mausoleums

Large scale mausoleums of the *Tokugawa* family were constructed in *Zōjōji* Temple in the Edo period. The tomb of a *Shōgun* remains intact and available for viewing.

● 山王日枝神社

SANNŌ-HIÉ SHRINE

● **Chiyoda Subway Line / 5 min. northwest of Akasaka Sta.**

This shrine was originally built in 830. In the Edo period, it was the site of worship for the *Ubusuna* god, protector of the birth place of the *Tokugawa* family. It enjoyed the auspicious position of being the biggest of all the shrines in Edo city.

Sannō Shintō Archway
While all *shintō* shrines are known for the archway that stands in their entrance, the one at the *Sannō-Hié* Shrine is particularly characterized by its unique triangle shaped roof.

The interior of the Shaden, or Main Sanctuary

A statue of a female monkey holding her off-spring serves as a symbol of marital harmony and safe childbirth within the temple compounds.

Sannō Festival (Held from 10 – 16, June)

The featured attraction of this festival is found in the *Hommatsuri*, or Main Festival held every other year. This event was also known as the "Festival Without Equal" during the Edo period.

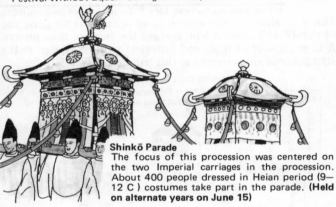

Shinkō Parade

The focus of this procession was centered on the two Imperial carriages in the procession. About 400 people dressed in Heian period (9–12 C) costumes take part in the parade. **(Held on alternate years on June 15)**

Miko Kagura Sacred Music

Sannō Hié Shrine Maidens hold performances of sacred dance and music offered to the shrine deity.

Chigaya Shintō Ritual

People pass through a large ring woven out of *Chigaya*, or Alang grass, in the belief that this ritual will grant them a year of happiness.

● 泉岳寺

SENGAKUJI TEMPLE

● Toei Asakusa Subway Line / 2 min. west of Sengakuji Sta.

This is a celebrated site known to all in Japan as the grave site of the 47 *Akō Samurai* who avenged the death of their master. A large number of relics and historical artifacts related to the *Akō Samurai* are preserved at this temple.

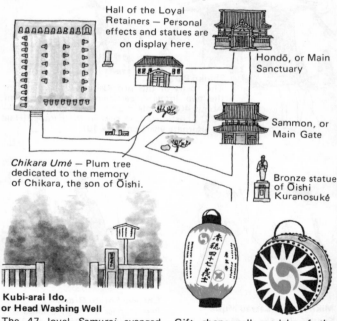

Hall of the Loyal Retainers — Personal effects and statues are on display here.

Hondō, or Main Sanctuary

Sammon, or Main Gate

Chikara Umé — Plum tree dedicated to the memory of Chikara, the son of Ōishi.

Bronze statue of Ōishi Kuranosuké

Kubi-arai Ido, or Head Washing Well

The 47 loyal *Samurai* avenged their master by beheading his enemy. It is said that the severed head was washed here.

Gift shops sell models of the drums used by the *Akō* retainers as well as paper lanterns upon which their names are written.

The Story of the Chūshingura Retainers

Resentful of the unfortunate circumstances surrounding the forced suicide *(seppuku)* of their lord, these 47 loyal retainers spent over two years to avenge his death. The historical events from this tale form the basis of the famous *Kabuki* play, *"Kanadehon Chūshingura"*.

The feudal lord of the *Akō* clan, *Asano Naganori*, unable to endure the taunting insults of *Kira Kōzukenosuké*, was provoked into assaulting him within the quarters of Edo Castle (see p. 14,15).

Asano was ordered to commit *seppuku* (ritual suicide) for his serious breach of behaviour within the confines of Edo Castle where drawing one's sword was forbidden. *Kira Kōzukenosuké,* on the other hand, was found completely innocent.

Deprived of their master, the *samurai* of the *Akō* clan had been disbanded before regrouping behind *Ōishi Kuranosuké*. Overcoming great odds they ultimately avenged their master's tragic demise.

The 47 *Akō samurai* involved in this 1702 incident were ordered to commit *seppuku* the following year although they had the popular support of the common people.

浮世絵
UKIYO-É

Ukiyo-é are pictures depicting Edo customs and fashions using the wood block printing techniques of the times. The motif of these prints dealt with Edo Ladies, *Kabuki* Actors, *Sumō* Wrestlers and various other scenes. They have provided us with a fair amount of information about the habits and customs of that time period.

Katsushika Hokusai was a celebrated artist particularly noted for his interpretations of various angles of Mt. Fuji in his series, "The Thirty-six Views of Mt. Fuji"

One of the distinctive features of the prints of Edo Ladies and *Kabuki* Actors were their caricaturized facial qualities. These particular types of *Ukiyo-é* were often used to decorate Japanese Battledores. (see p. 39)

The Ukiyo-é Production Process

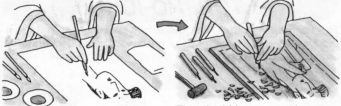

The *eshi,* or painter, draws the design on the paper.

The *horishi,* or wood carver, chisels out the form on the wood block.

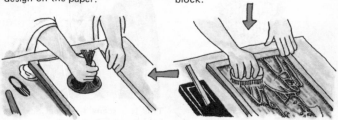

The print is then made using a *baren,* a tool for pressing.

The *surishi,* or printer, uses a brush to apply color to the wood block.

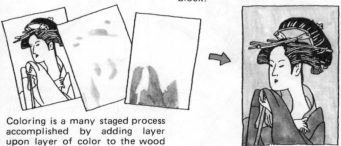

Coloring is a many staged process accomplished by adding layer upon layer of color to the wood block print.

TORI-NO-ICHI

This fair is held at the Ōtori Shrine in Asakusa in November on the Day of the Rooster in the old lunar calendar method of reckoning. Many people attend this event seeking good fortune in the following year.

This is a scene from a Cock fair held in the Edo period.

Kazari Kumadé — decorated bamboo rakes

Many colorful bamboo rakes decorated with all sorts of good luck charms are sold at the Cock fair. Some people believe that these objects bought at the fair will help them "rake in" fortune and happiness.

EARLY MODERN TOKYO

imperial palace·hibiya
kasumigaseki·shimbashi
opening the city to western
influence

THE IMPERIAL PALACE

● **Chiyoda Subway Line/ 5 min. west of Nijūbashi-maé Sta**.

The Imperial Palace situated right in the heart of Tokyo was formerly Edo Castle, the headquarters of the *Tokugawa* Shogunate. At the end of the *Meiji* Restoration it was established as the official residence of Emperor *Meiji* and was originally called Tokyo Castle. This was the designated name for a long period of time until it later became known as *Kōkyo*, or the Imperial Palace.

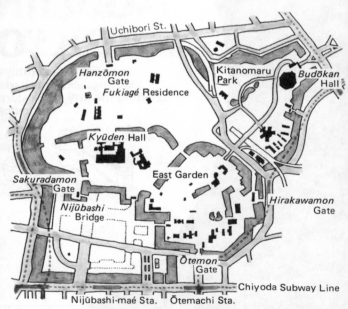

Within the Imperial Palace, vestiges of the former Edo Castle remain in the form of many stone fortress walls and immense protective gates.

Nijūbashi Bridge

Former bridge

Present structure of the Shakkyō Bridge (Megané-bashi)

Nijūbashi Bridge, or the Double Bridge, would seem to be an obvious name for the two bridges adjacent to each other. One of them is made out of steel. The other, a stone structure, is known as a *megané-bashi*, or eyeglass bridge. In fact, the name, "Double Bridge", is derived from the predecessor of the steel bridge. A wooden structure with an upper and a lower level, this former bridge was aptly referred to as a "double bridge". Although this double decker structure was destroyed, its name survived to assume a different meaning.

Sakuradamon Gate

A defensive measure taken against attack was attained in the use of the *Masugatamon*, a square-shaped outer courtyard. This construction can be seen at the *Sakuradamon* Gate.

The *Sakuradamon* Gate is well-known as the site of the assassination of Lord *Ii Naosuké*, Chief Minister of the *Shōgun* in 1860, by a splinter group of a clan trying to topple the Shogunate.

The Stone Wall of The Fujimi Turret

The personal mark of a mason who undertook the construction of this one wall of the Edo Castle is carved into the rock.

Remanents of Gun Emplacements Near The Hirakawamon Gate

This stone wall built with emplacements to enable the defenders to hold rifles easily at the ready has been kept in a good state of repair.

Various types of Stone Wall Masonry

Nozura Style

Arranging uncut quarry stones in the wall.

Uchikomi Style

Trimming the corners of stones. All edges are made to fit snugly one against the other.

Kirikomi Style

Each stone is cut into a square shape and laid to avoid any openings between stones.

Construction of the *Kyūden* Hall was completed in October 1968. State functions of the Imperial Household are held here.

Formal events such as the arrival of a State Guest, New Year's celebrations or the birthday of the Emperor, are hosted at Imperial Dinner Banquets held at *Hōmeiden* Hall.

Court Entrance

Inner Garden

Seiden

South Garden

Center Garden

Hōmeiden Hall

Chōwaden Hall

Kyūden Hall

The *Seiden Matsu-no-Ma* where the Emperor and Empress along with the rest of the Imperial Family accept the best wishes for the New Year from the Prime Minister, high government officials and others.

The general public has an opportunity to meet the Imperial Family twice a year when the inner section of the Imperial Palace is opened for congratulatory visits on January 2 and the Emperor's Birthday on December 23. Standing on the *Chōwaden* Balcony, the Imperial Family are happy to receive greetings from visitors. The times for these two events are from 9:30 a.m. to 3:00 p.m. on January 2 and in the morning on December 23.

Hinomaru (National flag)

Commoners Visit to The Imperial Palace

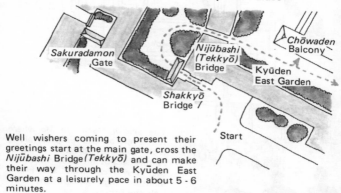

Sakuradamon Gate

Nijūbashi (Tekkyō) Bridge

Chōwaden Balcony

Kyūden East Garden

Shakkyō Bridge

Start

Well wishers coming to present their greetings start at the main gate, cross the *Nijūbashi* Bridge *(Tekkyō)* and can make their way through the Kyūden East Garden at a leisurely pace in about 5 - 6 minutes.

The wide promenade circling the deep moat of the Imperial Palace has become an area noted for use as a running course. One lap around the moat is 5 km. The course can be extended to a little less than 6 km by passing around the *Kitanomaru* Park. Although the promenade can be freely used by joggers, those wishing to hold marathon races should apply for a permit at the Imperial Outer Garden Management Office (Telephone: 213-0095). Furthermore, a permit for road use must be issued by the Marunouchi Police Department.

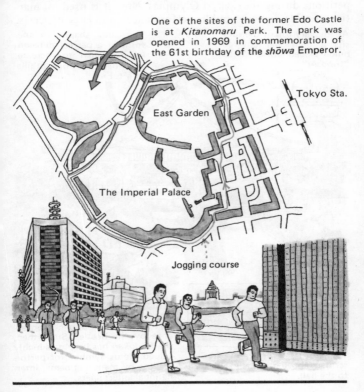

One of the sites of the former Edo Castle is at *Kitanomaru* Park. The park was opened in 1969 in commemoration of the 61st birthday of the *shōwa* Emperor.

Tokyo Sta.

East Garden

The Imperial Palace

Jogging course

BUDŌKAN HALL

● Tōzai Subway Line/5 min. west of Kudanshita Sta.

The Japan Martial Arts Hall known as *Budōkan* is located in *Kitanomaru* Park. It was built in 1964 for use in the *Jūdō* competitions during the Tokyo Olympics. Now it is used for martial art athletic meets, public performances, and large concerts.

At the very top of the roof sits a gold leaf covered onion-shaped form called "Giboshi"

5.15m 3.35m
1.8m

The roof shaped in the form of a perfect octagon was designed to recreate the image of the foothills of Mt. Fuji.

The words, "Budōkan", are inscribed above the main entrance to the hall.

The hall was first used for a concert in 1968 in a public appearance by the Beatles. Since then, the *Budōkan* has become a highly valued status symbol for performances by many big name, international entertainers.

Japanese Martial Arts

The main objectives of the *Budōkan* have been the popularization and advancement of the various forms of martial arts. Among the list of events it has hosted are competitions of *Jūdō, Kendō, Kyūdō, Aikidō, Karaté, Naginata,* and *Shōrinji-Kempō.*

Jūdō

In 1882 a martial arts master, Kanō Jigorō, first taught the principals of *Jūdō* with the establishment of his *Kōdōkan* practice hall.

Kanō Jigorō

Nagé-waza

Katamé-waza

When a decision has been reached in a bout, the word "*Ippon*" is called indicating a winner.

Kendō

Long ago, the *Bushi* warriors used Japanese swords as weapons in battle. *Kendō* was the first martial art to promote both the mental and physical development that resulted in the pursuit of perfection in the way of the Japanese sword.

Shinai — a bamboo sword

Koté — an arm protector

Men — mask

Dō — Chest protector

Taré — protective apron

Victory is determined by striking the opponent in either the *Men,* the *Koté,* or the *Dō.* Both physical and mental force, as well as fighting form, are among the criteria for selecting the winner.

● 国会議事堂

JAPANESE DIET BUILDING

● Marunouchi Subway Line/2 min. of Kokkai-gijidōmaé Sta.

The Japanese legislative system usually referred to as the Diet, is a two chamber system consisting of a House of Councilors and a House of Representatives. The Diet building is the sanctuary of this one form of democratic government. Beginning in 1920, construction of this granite covered pyramidal structure spanned a 17 year period before its completion in 1937.

House of Representatives
511 members

House of Councilors
252 members

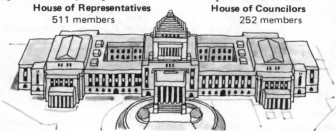

A total of 9,810 tons of steel beams were used in the construction of the Diet building. About 5,522 tons of steel rods, 1.2 cm in diameter, were also used. If these rods were placed end to end, they would make a 6,220 km line comparable to the distance from *Tokyo* to *Honolulu*.

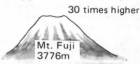

30 times higher

Mt. Fuji
3776m

Over 377,926 slabs of stone materials (primarily granite and marble) weighing 28,406 tons were used in the Diet building. If each of these slabs were piled up one on the other, they would reach a height over thirty times that of Mt. Fuji.

The combined work force involved in the structural, mechanical and electrical work amounted to 2,542,877 people.

Tokyo

6220km

Honolulu

The seating arrangements of members of all political factions in the plenary session is decided in individual council meetings. After the seating arrangements of important figures of each political party are completed, a number of ballots are drawn to determine who occupies the remaining seats. A special seating gallery called the *Hinadan*, or The Doll Shelf is relegated to the Prime Minister and his Cabinet members.

Name Plate

Indication of an absent Diet member

Participating member

Diet members never fail to wear this pin which wields tremendous authority in Japanese society.

The marron colored pin of members of the House of Representatives.

The deep purple pin of the House of Councilors.

● 霞が関

KASUMIGASEKI

Kasumigaseki is the area bordering the south side of the Imperial Palace. The Ministries of Justice, Foreign Affairs, the Treasury, International Trade and Industry are among the new and old buildings of 30 central government agencies concentrated in an area on both sides of *Sakurada* Street. This area has clearly become the administrative center of the Japanese National Government.

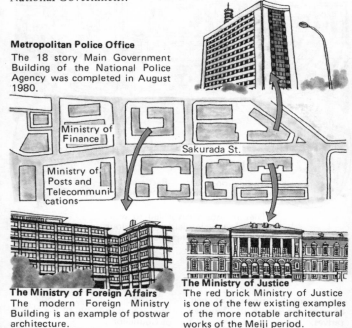

Metropolitan Police Office
The 18 story Main Government Building of the National Police Agency was completed in August 1980.

Ministry of Finance

Ministry of Posts and Telecommunications

Sakurada St.

The Ministry of Foreign Affairs
The modern Foreign Ministry Building is an example of postwar architecture.

The Ministry of Justice
The red brick Ministry of Justice is one of the few existing examples of the more notable architectural works of the Meiji period.

● 浜離宮

HAMARIKYŪ GARDEN

● JR Yamanoté Line/15 min. southeast of Shimbashi Sta.

At the edge of *Shimbashi* facing the *Shiodomé* district area is a familiar seaside park known as *Hamarikyū*. The ebb and flow of the tide empties and fills a pond in the park, creating a constantly changing atmosphere to this natural setting. In the Edo period this park served as a villa for the *Tokugawa* family. Following the end of World War ll, it was opened for admission to the general public.

This spot served as the disembarkation point for the *Shōgun* after boating excursions on the *Sumida* River.

A floodgate was built in order to preserve the charm of the garden by regulating the level of sea water filling the pond.

Disembarkation point for the Shōgun

Water gate

Landing Pier of Water Buses

This has become a landing and departure pier for two boat tours: one on the *Sumida* River line and another on the Maritime Science Museum Line.

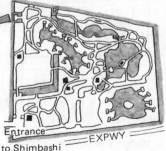

● 日比谷
HIBIYA

● Toei Mita Subway Line/Near Hibiya Sta.

Hibiya Park opened in 1903 as the first western style park in Japan. The total surface covers a 159,887 m² area. Along with adjacent Imperial palace this park serves as an urban oasis. It is also well known as a popular spot for couples to stroll on a date.

Outdoor Music Hall

Jazz, Rock, Folk and other types of concerts are held in this facility which is very popular among young people.

Matsumotorō Restaurant

This restaurant opened in the same year as the park. At that time it was considered quite fashionable to come here for Indian curry or coffee. A ten yen curry meal for charity is held every year on September 25.

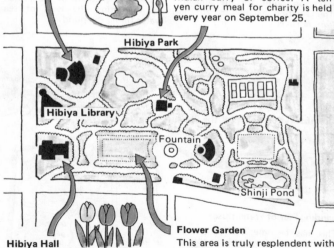

Hibiya Hall

This music hall has been designed in Modern Gothic style.

Flower Garden

This area is truly resplendent with seasonal flowers. The tulips are considered the most lovely in all of Tokyo.

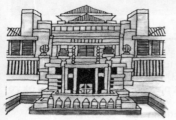

The former Imperial Hotel

This structure has been preserved in *Meiji* Village in *Inuyama* City in *Aichi* Prefecture.

A Short History of the Imperial Hotel

In 1884, *Inoue Kaoru* (the Foreign Minister) built *Rokumei-kan* Hall as a place for social gatherings. The cream of Japanese high society and the foreign community were invited there. In 1890, *Inoue* proposed construction of the Imperial Hotel adjacent to the north side of the *Rokumei-kan* Hall. Destroyed by fire, the Imperial Hotel was rebuilt by the famous American architect, *Frank Lloyd Wright*. After having far surpassed its life span, it was completely razed in 1968. The present structure is a 17 story high building acknowledged as a truly first class hotel.

Rokumei-kan Hall was torn down in 1940 without any trace of the original structure.

A typical evening ballroom scene of fashionable high society is shown at *Rokumei-kan* Hall.

TOKYO STATION

Tokyo Station is the terminal station of Japan in every sense of the word. A combination of nine different public trains and subways make for a total of 3,000 arrivals a day into the station. About 700,000 passengers pass through the Grand Tokyo main entrance of the station where a total of twelve train platforms can be found on 5 underground levels.

As a large central terminal for so many arrivals and departures, people in Japan tend to consider all trains leading to Tokyo station as "heading up" to the city regardless of their geographical point of orientation.

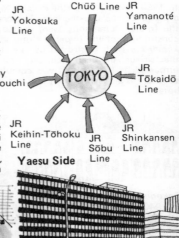

JR Chūō Line
JR Yokosuka Line
JR Yamanoté Line
Subway Marunouchi Line
TOKYO
JR Tōkaidō Line
JR Keihin-Tōhoku Line
JR Sōbu Line
JR Shinkansen Line

Marunouchi Side

Tokyo station is epitomized by the red brick Renaissance style architecture of the Marunouchi entrance. Modeled after the central station in Amsterdam, construction was completed in 1914.

Yaesu Side

In sharp contrast to the Marunouchi side of the station, a modern shopping center station building can be found at the Yaesu entrance.

MARUNOUCHI · ŌTEMACHI

The Marunouchi district was the site of the mansion of a *daimyō*, a feudal lord during the Edo period. This area quickly expanded along with the opening of Tokyo station in 1914. Now the long towering rows of trading companies, banks and large enterprises serve as the business center driving the economy of Japan.

Marunouchi-Building

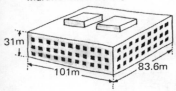

31m
101m
83.6m

Just next to the Marunouchi side of Tokyo station stands the *Marunouchi* Building which was a symbol of the prewar Marunouchi district. A well-known structure in the heart of the city, it's cubic surface was once the standard of measurement in times of flooding or excessive rain fall.

At lunch time the shopping area corridors of these busy office buildings become pedestrian malls for the businessman. Restaurants do a brisk business with "Lunch Special" prices cheaper than at other times.

Hamburger Steak Lunch

vegetables

Hamburger steak

Pickled vegetables

Rice

Miso soup

NATIONAL NOH THEATER

● **JR Chūō Line/10 min. west of Sendagaya Sta.**

Noh, considered the oldest traditional art form, is a kind of Japanese-style opera focusing on masked performers on stage. There are five distinct schools of *Noh* Drama. Although these schools of *Noh* have their own stages for performances, National *Noh* Theater, completed in 1983, is the one place where the productions of all the schools of *Noh* Drama can be seen.

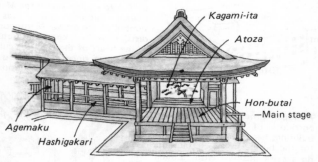

Kagami-ita

Atoza

Hon-butai —Main stage

Agemaku

Hashigakari

Tsuzumi

The musical accompaniment of *Noh* consists of a wind instrument called a *Nohkan* and percussion instruments: *Tsuzumi* and *Taiko*.

Nohkan

Taiko

Noh Costumes

An assortment of various types of costumes indicate the identity, sex, age and role of the members of the cast.

Noh-men
—Mask

Karaori

The costumes worn by actors playing female roles or young court nobles are distinguished by the use of a special weave of cloth known as *Karaori*.

Folding fan

Noh Masks

The roles of all characters in *Noh* dramas are performed by male actors. The leading actor is called *shité*. The supporting actor is *waki*. Characters represented in the role of the *shité* are living human figures, deities or the spirits of the departed. The *Noh* mask epitomizes the subtlety of *form* characteristic of *Noh* drama. Depending on the angle and movement of the *Noh* mask, the actor can convey a wide range of emotion from joy to sorrow.

Kobeshimi
A male evil spirit

Hannya
A female evil spirit

Kojō
An old man

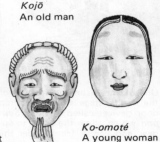

Ko-omoté
A young woman

● 歌舞伎座

KABUKIZA THEATER

● **Hibiya Subway Line/Near Higashi-ginza Sta.**

This theater used exclusively for *Kabuki* performances was built in 1889. The unmistakable Japanese style gabled roof structure indicates to all where the sanctuary of the *Kabuki* art form is located. It's reputation is well established both in Japan and abroad.

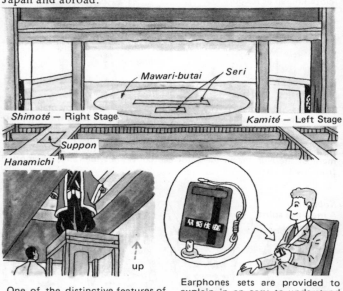

Mawari-butai *Seri*

Shimoté — Right Stage

Kamité — Left Stage

Suppon

Hanamichi

↑ up

One of the distinctive features of the *Kabuki* stage is the use of trap door devices called *Seri* and *Suppon* which allow the actor to appear and vanish from under the floor of the stage.

Earphones sets are provided to explain in an easy to understand manner all aspects of a *Kabuki* scene from the storyline to the actors or even the music. An English language version is also available.

104

Sajiki-seki

Gallery box seats are furnished with *tatami* mats. The *tatami* matting is specially designed to permit the theater goer to sit western-style, thus creating a spacious and comfortable setting. At the intermission food and drink are served.

Counter-style Table
Hot Water Warmer
Oshibori — or wet towel
Tatami chair
Tatami floor cushion

It is possible to make arrangements to reserve a *Makunouchi*-lunch. Delivery of the box lunch to the theater goer is made just prior to the fall of the curtain at intermission time.

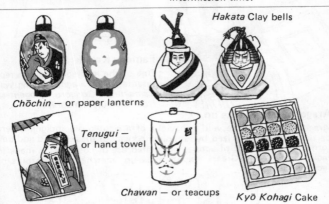

Hakata Clay bells

Chōchin — or paper lanterns

Tenugui — or hand towel

Chawan — or teacups

Kyō Kohagi Cake

A wide range of shops within the *Kabukiza* theater sell all kinds of souvenirs: dolls, tea cups, confectionery, items related to *Kabuki,* and many kinds of traditional Japanese goods.

歌舞伎

KABUKI

Kabuki is representative of Japanese traditional performing arts along with *Noh*, *Kyōgen* and *Bunraku*. This art form was first performed by an all female troupe of *Kabuki* actors lead by *Izumo-no-Okuni* in 17 C. This later developed into an exclusively male theater troupe performance. It has continued up to the present in this form.

Ōdachi

Gohon-kuruma-bin

Niō-dasuki

Ōsuō

Famous Kabuki Scenes

One of the leading characters representative of *aragoto* acting was *Kamakura - Gongoro - Kagemasa* from the play, *Shibaraku*.

Aragoto Facial Make up

Aragoto indicates the wild behaviour of a righteously indignant hero particularly characterized by his animated way of speaking. To add uniformity to this style of acting, exaggerated use of cosmetics is made in facial preparation. Grease paint make-up matches the contours of face muscles.

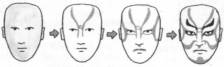

Oyama

In *Kabuki* women's role are played by male actors. The roles of actors who dress up to impersonate woman are called *Oyama*.

Mié-o-kiru
The grandiose use of bigger than life gestures is considered the most impressive of all Kabuki acting techniques.

Nimaimé
This is a handsome young man. (*Sammaimé* is the name given to clowns.)

Keren-mi
The acting technique makes an actor appear deceptive, using tricky and wily gestures.

Tachimawari
The presentation of a fight scene is in choreographical form.

Jūhachiban
The 18 most enjoyable plays representative of the *Kabuki* art form are used to convey the meaning of a successful performance.

Daté-otoko
This is a *saké* drinking, easily angered, but agreeable man who is well liked by women.

The names of some particularly distinctive techniques and movements used in *Kabuki* acting have been carried over into the everyday world. These words are used to describe certain behaviour and personality types in contemporary society.

Janomé-gasa

Hachimaki

Wakizashi

The proud pose of the *Daté-otoko* is shown by the *Sukeroku* from the play, *Sukeroku-yukari-no-edozakura*.

• 迎賓館
GEIHINKAN

• **JR Chūō Line/7 min. south of Yotsuya Sta.**

The State Guesthouse was established to accommodate foreign dignitaries. Completed at the end of the Meiji period, the *Tōgū* Palace was a western-style structure modeled after the Versailles Palace. Having undergone major rennovations in 1974, it was reborn as the *Geihinkan,* or State Guesthouse. Since then, it has hosted top level dignitaries, the likes of which include Lady Diana, American presidents and various world leaders.

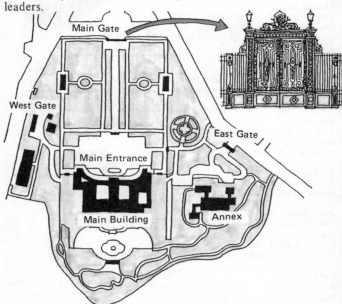

The interior of the State Guesthouse has been lavishly furnished with ceiling murals, rich carpeting, elegant furniture, decorative tiles, chandeliers and other sorts of artistic ornamentation. No effort has been spared to adorn this building with the very best that contemporary art has to offer.

The Main Building

The reception room, Hagoromo-no-ma

A grand ceiling mural depicts the *Noh* world of the "robe of feathers"

The chandelier is the largest of all the art objects in the State Guest house.

Furnishings are done in late 18 C French style

RYŌTEI・GEISHA

Ryōtei restaurants are considered high class establishments catering to connoisseurs of traditional Japanese cuisine. The *Ryōtei* is a place where receptions, important closed door consultations and business negotiations are held.

The usual patrons tend to come from the upper levels of governments, the financial community or executives of large scale enterprises.

Kakejiku
— a hanging scroll

Japanese garden

Toko-no-ma
— an alcove

visitor

The design of these restaurants is always in a subdued Japanese style free of gaudy signs or flashy neon lights.

When one thinks of *Ryōtei* restaurants, the image of *Geisha* always seems to come to mind. From early childhood *Geisha* train hard to acquire skill in singing old songs to the accompaniment of a *samisen*, performing traditional Japanese dances and various other performing arts. Before coming of age as a *Geisha, hangyoku,* or young apprentice *Geisha*, are summoned to a banquet to perform various functions such as announcing the start of a performance, animating the mood of the gathering or calming things down in the course of events.

These *Geisha* are attached to an *Okiya,* or *Geisha* house. The *Geisha* proceed to the *Ryōtei* restaurants from this residence. The fee charged for the services of these *Geisha* are referred to as "Flower Money", "Pocket Money" or "Incense Money". The name varies according to the *Ryōtei* restaurant.

The top level *Geisha* are found in the Akasaka area. All other ranks are concentrated in Shinbashi, Kagurazaka, Nihonbashi, Asakusa, Itabashi and various other places.

Japanese coiffure

Obi—belt

Kimono

Sensu
— Folding fan

Shafu

The wheeled carriage drawn by a person is called *Jinrikisha*.
Although their use was at its peak during the Meiji period, with the advent of the train, automobile and other forms of conveyance, the number of *Jinrikisha* decreased little by little. Now, only a limited number of them can be seen in the vicinity of red light districts.

EDO STYLE CUISINE [3]

Originally *Kaiseki* cooking was developed as an integral part of the art of tea ceremony. A highly refined style of cuisine, in its present day form it is offered at *Ryōtei* restaurants and other establishments catering to discriminating tastes.

FULL KAISEKI COURSE:

Yutō (hot water with scorched rice)

Matcha (powdered green tea)

Yakimono (grilled fish)

Hashiarai (light soup)

Wammori (main dish, meat or fish with vegetables and garnishes in clear soup)

Shiizakana (accompaniment to *saké*)

Mukōzuké (side dish, usually raw seafood)

Hassun (All sorts of delicacies on a square tray)

Meshi (rice)

Shiru (miso soup)

Great importance is placed on the preparation of *Kaiseki* cuisine in conformity to spiritual notions associated with the tea ceremony. In particular, the concepts of *wabi*, or quiet simplicity and *sabi*, or unstudied elegance are reflected in the artistic preparation of a *Kaiseki* meal.

Japanese Table Manners

Japanese food is usually eaten with chopsticks. One hand is used to hold the chopstick while the other is for holding the various dishes.

Chopsticks are held with the narrow end facing away from the user. The upper stick is moved in order to grasp food.

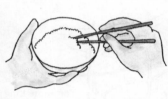

Japanese plates are expressly designed to be held easily in one hand. Rice and soup are eaten by bringing the bowl up towards one's mouth.

The small dish used for soy sauce or broth when eating *Tempura* or *Sushi* is supported with one's hand while eating.

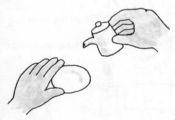

Pour only the necessary amount of soy sauce in the small dish.

When the meal is completed, place the chopsticks and bowls with lids on them back into their original positions.

●明治神宮
MEIJI JINGŪ SHRINE

● **JR Yamanoté Line/Near Harajuku Sta.**

The *Meiji Jingū* Shrine is consecrated to the Emperor *Meiji* and the Empress Dowager *Shōken*. The shrine compound with its many trees and bushes creates a dense forest right in the center of the city. No other shrine in all of Japan receives as many people for the *Hatsumōdé*, or first visit of the New Year as the *Meiji Jingū* shrine. In matter of fact, in 1986, 2,412,250 people came on New Year's Day alone.

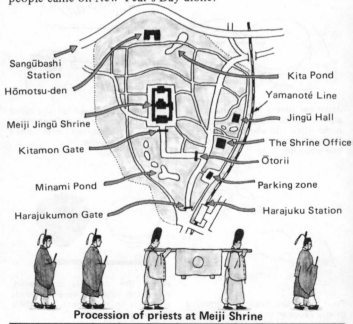

Procession of priests at Meiji Shrine

Honden and Ōtorii

Chigi

Katsuogi

One of the structures of the shrine, the *Honden*, or main sanctuary, was built in *Nagaré-zukuri* style architecture. The Great Shintō Archway boasts of being the largest wooden one in all of Japan

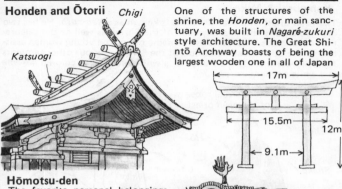

17m

15.5m

12m

9.1m

Hōmotsu-den

The favorite personal belongings of Emperor *Meiji* and Empress Dowager *Shōken* are contained here.

The carriage was drawn by a team of six horses used in the Constitution Proclamation Ceremony in 1889.

Emperor *Meiji*, concerned about the disintegration of traditional Japanese morals due to the influence of western civilization, issued this book on public morals in 1881.

This Indian inkstone case was made from bamboo in *Kagoshima* Prefecture.

The elegance of this *Meiji* period garden has been faithfully preserved. Among the many lovely features of the garden are the irises which appear in all their glory in June.

Kan-nushi & Miko

The head priest of a *Shintō* Shrine is known as a *Kan-nushi*. He has two main functions: the management of the Shrine as well as the celebration of religious rites. *Miko* is the name given to a young woman assisting in the day to day operation of the Shrine. Various other garments for daily use include the *Kariginu*, a white robe with a colored *hakama* and white garment called a *Jōi*.

Ikan — the formal robes of the head priest.

Eboshi

Hō

Shaku

Asagutsu

Kan-nushi

Noshi

Chihaya

Hibakama

Miko

Shichi-go-san

7

5

3

Chitose-amé stick shaped candy in decorated paper bags.

Shichi-go-san is a festival to celebrate the growth of children at the ages of three, five and seven. Parents accompany their children to the shrine for this event to pray for their continued good health and fortune. *Meiji Jingū* Shrine is the scene of numerous children dressed in brightly-colored *Kimono* or western-style, formal clothing and paraded about by proud parents. This ceremony is held every year on November 15.

There are many distinctively Shintoist practices and charms to be found when visiting a Shrine. These various objects are used by worshippers as a means of communicating with the gods or to ask them for protection from some evil or misfortune.

① Using a laddle, water is poured over the left and right hands.

Chōzu is the act of spiritual purification using water before worship at the shrine.

② Taking water drawn by the laddle into the palm of one hand, the mouth is rinsed out.

③ Finally the laddle is returned to its original resting position.

Shintō religious charms

Omamori: a charm believed to possess mysterious powers protecting one from evil forces and inviting good fortune.

Omikuji: a form of fortune-telling in which divine will is revealed on randomnly selected slips of papers.

Ema: a votive wooden tablet on which one's prayers are written.

●新橋

SHIMBASHI

Shimbashi is the zone that follows the Ginza area in the north east edge of Minato ward. It developed as one of the busiest parts of town after the very first railroad terminal was established at Shimbashi station. The first steam locomotive train in Japan ran from Shimbashi Station to Yokohama in 1872. For this reason Shimbashi is also called the birth place of the Japanese railroad.

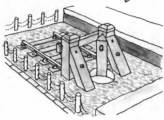

The location of Shimbashi station was moved in 1924. The site where it first started service is now known as the *Shiodomé* Freight Station. Preserved within the railyard compound are the terminal point of the train line indicated by the original "0 mile" marker along with a part of the track and the platform from that period.

Old Engine Number One

The former *Shimbashi-Yokohama* 29 km line made a one way run in 53 minutes for a total of 9 round trips in a day. Old Engine Number One had 10 cars and weighed 25 tons. It was a small locomotive with a 300 horse-power engine.

A 1945 Steam Locomotive Train has been set up in the square in front of Shimbashi station to commemorate the 100 anniversary of the innauguration of rail service in Japan.

In the Edo period *Karasumori* at the west entrance to the station, was a town crammed with red lanterns hanging from meeting places and *Geisha* Shops. This reputation has survived in the form of various drinking spots, small restaurants and other sundry shops in the small alleyways of that area. At night it becomes a haven for all sorts of people looking for an escape from the cares of the working world.

• 都電

THE MUNICIPAL STREET CAR SYSTEM

Toden was the name given to the streetcars which ran within the central Tokyo area. At one time there were 41 lines criss-crossing the central area like the meshes of a net. However, the only remaining line in existence is the *Arakawa* Line running from the Waseda district of Shinjuku Ward to Minowabashi in Arakawa Ward.

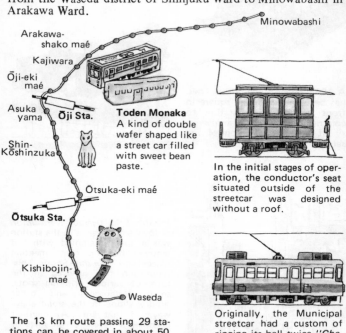

Minowabashi

Arakawa-shako maé

Kajiwara

Ōji-eki maé

Asuka yama   **Ōji Sta.**

Shin-Kōshinzuka

Toden Monaka
A kind of double wafer shaped like a street car filled with sweet bean paste.

In the initial stages of operation, the conductor's seat situated outside of the streetcar was designed without a roof.

Ōtsuka-eki maé

Ōtsuka Sta.

Kishibojin-maé

Waseda

The 13 km route passing 29 stations can be covered in about 50 minutes traveling at an average speed of 25 km/h.

Originally, the Municipal streetcar had a custom of ringing its bell twice "Che-en Cheen!" before leaving a station.

120

Ōji Inari Shrine

The *Ōji Inari* Shrine has been in existence since 10 C. In the Edo period the Shogunate family would come here to make their supplications. The present *Honden*, or Main Sanctuary, was built in 1808.

The *Inari* is one category of Shrine protected by a guardian deity in the form of a fox.

Shibaraku Kitsuné Fox

The *Ōji Inari* Shrine sells an Edo play thing called the *Shibaraku Kitsuné* Fox. The creation of this toy is attributed to a *Kabuki* actor who came to the Ōji Inari Shrine to pray for the success of the play, "*Shibaraku*" (see p.106).

The toy fox waves its paw when a bamboo stick attached underneath is moved up and down.

Zōshigaya Kishibojin

An unusual form of folk craft, the *Susuki Mimizuku* Horned Owl is sold here.

The guardian deity of children called *Kishibojin* is enshrined here. The present structure was built in 1666.

KAPPABASHI

Kappabashi Street near Asakusa is a well known wholesale shopping area for restaurant cooking utensils. Pots, pans and all other types of items are sold. The most unusual items, however, are found among the large assortment of wax food replicas that look just like the real thing.

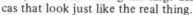

About 188 stores are lined along the 800 meters of this shopping street. One of these stores stands out from all the rest with a large scale model of the head of a chef placed on the roof.

These food sample replicas which appear in restaurant shop windows range in size and style from *sushi, soba* noodles, and curry rice to elaborate ceremonial wedding cakes.

The price of all these replicas usually amount to about ten times the cost of the actual item they represent.

PRESENT DAY TOKYO

ginza·roppongi·shibuya
harajuku·shinjuku·aoyama
shaping the fashions and trends
of tomorrow

GINZA

The main throughfare of the Ginza district modeled after Regent street in London was the very first western style shopping promenade to be built in Japan. It is well known as a highly exclusive shopping district.

There are many picturesque old shops that have been in the hands of the same family since the Meiji period.

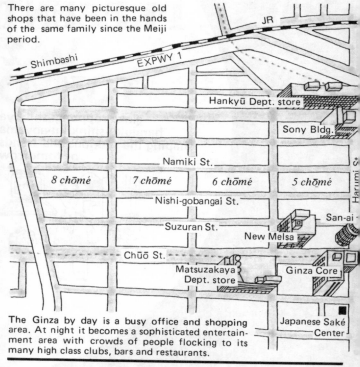

The Ginza by day is a busy office and shopping area. At night it becomes a sophisticated entertainment area with crowds of people flocking to its many high class clubs, bars and restaurants.

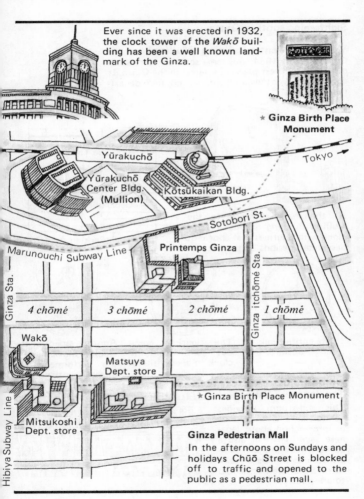

Ever since it was erected in 1932, the clock tower of the *Wakō* building has been a well known landmark of the Ginza.

★ **Ginza Birth Place Monument**

Yūrakuchō

Tokyo →

Yūrakuchō Center Bldg. (Mullion)

Kōtsūkaikan Bldg.

Sotobori St.

Marunouchi Subway Line

Printemps Ginza

Ginza Sta.

4 chōmé

3 chōmé

2 chōmé

Ginza itchōmé Sta.

1 chōmé

Wakō

Matsuya Dept. store

★ Ginza Birth Place Monument

Hibiya Subway Line

Mitsukoshi Dept. store

Ginza Pedestrian Mall

In the afternoons on Sundays and holidays Chūō Street is blocked off to traffic and opened to the public as a pedestrian mall.

Sightseeing spots in Ginza

Yūrakuchō Center Building (Mullion)

Completed in 1984, this large scale 14 story building is the newest place of interest in the Ginza. It consists of seven movie theaters, and two department stores.

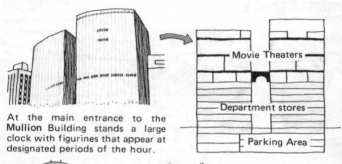

At the main entrance to the **Mullion** Building stands a large clock with figurines that appear at designated periods of the hour.

The entire clock moves upward.

The figurines come out from within the clock to greet visitors.

Another aspect of the clock's movement is the performance of musical instruments.

Nihonshu, or The Japanese Saké Center

This showroom provides connoisseurs with all kinds of information about Japanese *saké*. There is also a corner where one can sample various brands of *saké* to find the one best suited to one's taste.

126

The Ginza Subway Station

Three subway lines cross at the Ginza Subway Station. Underground passageways from Hibiya to Higashi-Ginza makes this one of the longest subway stations in all of Asia.

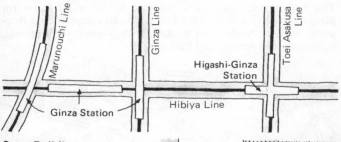

Sony Building

This building comprised of various showrooms, boutiques and restaurants is another Ginza landmark. A constant lineup of events are held right in front of the entrance on the first floor.

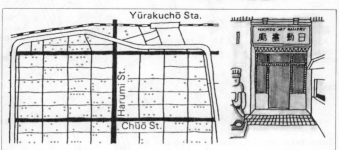

Art Galleries

The Ginza is recognized as having the world's largest number of art galleries (over 300) concentrated in any one area.

127

•六本木
ROPPONGI

This fashionable area takes the lead as the trend setter for progressive styles in modern living. The area surrounding Roppongi intersection is jam packed with innovative buildings, boutiques, restaurants and bars.

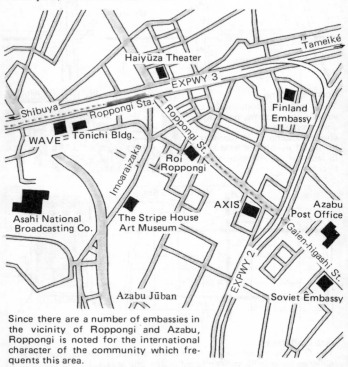

Since there are a number of embassies in the vicinity of Roppongi and Azabu, Roppongi is noted for the international character of the community which frequents this area.

The design of both the AXIS and WAVE buildings are based on new cultural concepts.

AXIS
Replete with an assortment of highly refined designs in cloth, furniture and kitchen utensils.

WAVE
The very first experiment in Japan of a building specializing in both sound and image.

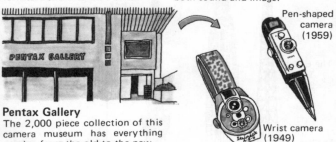

Pen-shaped camera (1959)

Wrist camera (1949)

Pentax Gallery
The 2,000 piece collection of this camera museum has everything ranging from the old to the new.

Roppongi is most notably known for its large number of discotheques.

129

TOKYO TOWER

● JR　Yamanoté Line / 15 min. west of Hamamatsuchō Sta.

Tokyo Tower is a 333 m high broadcasting antenna with an observation deck for sightseers. The distance of the tower to the observation deck alone makes it the highest in the world. Known as one of the more frequented points of interest in sightseeing tours of Tokyo.

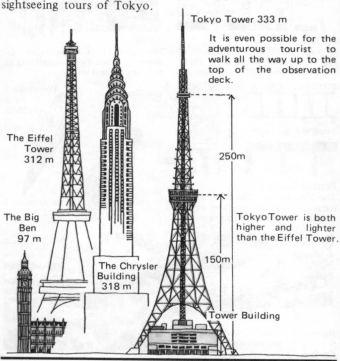

Tokyo Tower 333 m

It is even possible for the adventurous tourist to walk all the way up to the top of the observation deck.

The Eiffel Tower 312 m

The Big Ben 97 m

The Chrysler Building 318 m

250m

150m

Tokyo Tower is both higher and lighter than the Eiffel Tower.

Tower Building

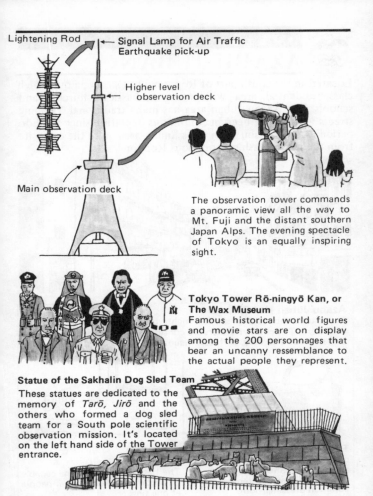

Lightening Rod

Signal Lamp for Air Traffic
Earthquake pick-up

Higher level
observation deck

Main observation deck

The observation tower commands a panoramic view all the way to Mt. Fuji and the distant southern Japan Alps. The evening spectacle of Tokyo is an equally inspiring sight.

Tokyo Tower Rō-ningyō Kan, or The Wax Museum

Famous historical world figures and movie stars are on display among the 200 personnages that bear an uncanny ressemblance to the actual people they represent.

Statue of the Sakhalin Dog Sled Team

These statues are dedicated to the memory of *Tarō, Jirō* and the others who formed a dog sled team for a South pole scientific observation mission. It's located on the left hand side of the Tower entrance.

•麻布十番
AZABU JŪBAN

Located in the south part of Roppongi lies Azabu, a quiet high class residential area with many embassies, churches and schools. The Azabu Jūban area has many traditional shopping streets which have been in continuous operation since the Edo period. All of Azabu is an unassuming area quite the opposite from the nearby fashion conscious Roppongi.

Azabu Jūban Hot Springs
This natural hot springs spa is a highly unusual site within the city of Tokyo. The curative waters are considered highly effective in trea ting nervous disorders, stiffness, rheumatism, and burns.

The hot springs spa has segregated communal bathing areas for men and women. Shoes are taken off outside. Clothes are removed in a common dressing room.

The bathtub is a large one capable of accommodating several people at one time.

Traditional Japanese Snacks available in the Azabu Jūban Area

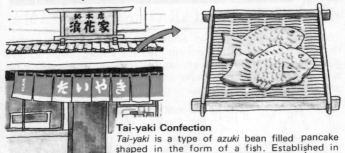

Tai-yaki Confection

Tai-yaki is a type of *azuki* bean filled pancake shaped in the form of a fish. Established in 1909, one particular *tai-yaki* specialty shop always has long lines of customers waiting outside.

Mamé Kashi, or Japanese Sweet Beans

This type of confection is made by boiling beans, adding a sugar coating then processing them in a number of other ways. In the Azabu Jūban area one shop demonstrates the confectionary process of these beans.

One big name confection shop in the Azabu Jūban area makes *Mizu-yōkan* and *Kuzu-zakura,* two kinds of Japanese jellies made from *azuki* bean paste.

●渋谷・原宿・青山
SHIBUYA·HARAJUKU & AOYAMA

The urban conglomerate of Shibuya, Harajuku and Aoyama is the most exciting entertainment area for young people today. Although the differences among the three areas appear to be minor, it is possible to observe a wide range of the latest trends and fashions of young Japanese people.

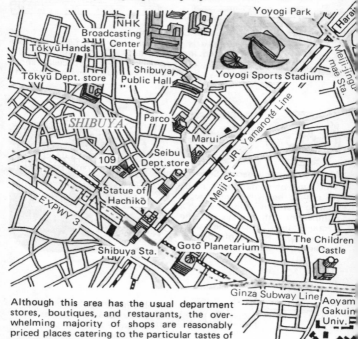

Although this area has the usual department stores, boutiques, and restaurants, the overwhelming majority of shops are reasonably priced places catering to the particular tastes of young people.

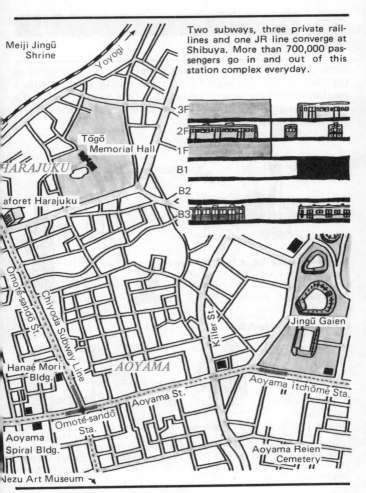

Two subways, three private rail-lines and one JR line converge at Shibuya. More than 700,000 passengers go in and out of this station complex everyday.

Meiji Jingū Shrine

Yoyogi

Tōgō Memorial Hall

3F
2F
1F
B1
B2
B3

HARAJUKU

aforet Harajuku

Omoté-sandō St.

Chiyoda Subway Line

Killer St.

AOYAMA

Jingū Gaien

Hanaé Mori Bldg.

Aoyama St.

Aoyama itchōme Sta.

Omoté-sandō Sta.

Aoyama Spiral Bldg.

Nezu Art Museum

Aoyama Reien Cemetery

●渋谷

SHIBUYA

Shibuya is considered by young people in their late teens as the place to go for a good time. People usually start off with a meal in one of the nearby restaurants then head to one of the many movies, fashion centers or department stores concentrated around Shibuya Station.

Statue of Hachikō, a faithful dog
Erected at the square in front of Shibuya Station, this famous area landmark is a popular meeting place.

The Story of Hachikō

In the 1920's, a university professor living in the Shibuya area kept an *Akita* dog. Every morning and evening this dog would come to the station to see off or meet his master.

Even after the death of his master in 1925, *Hachikō* continued to wait 11 years at Shibuya Station for a master who would never return.

136

Sightseeing Spots in Shibuya

Fashion Building

This Fashion building is not really a department store but a series of boutiques, record shops, and restaurants all incorporated into one grand building. In Shibuya there are many of these kinds of stores.

The Gotō Planetarium

Opened in 1957. The seasonal movement of constellations, the moon and other heavenly bodies is projected on a dome 20 m in diameter.

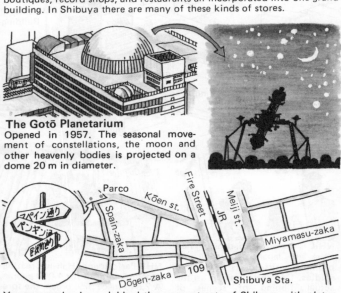

Young people have dubbed the many streets of Shibuya with picturesque names.

●NHK放送センター
NHK BROADCASTING CENTER

● **JR Yamanoté Line / 10 min. southwest of Harajuku Sta.**

Nippon Hōsō Kyōkai, or Japan Broadcasting Corporation, is a government operated agency consisting of a combined total of five domestic radio and television services. The overseas operations are directed to 18 worldwide zones in 21 languages.

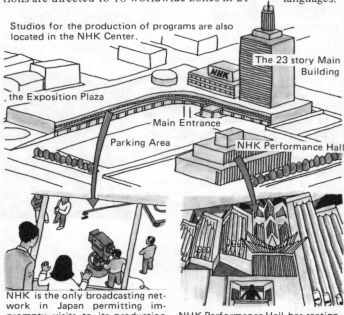

Studios for the production of programs are also located in the NHK Center.

The 23 story Main Building

the Exposition Plaza

Main Entrance

Parking Area

NHK Performance Hall

NHK is the only broadcasting network in Japan permitting impromptu visits to its production studios. One may look in on the actual filming of scenes of a program episode from the third floor.

NHK Performance Hall has seating accommodations for 4,000 people. A 7,640 piece pipe organ, the foremost in the world, has been installed.

Old Style Sound Effect Production Methods

Frog Croaking
Seashells were rubbed together to produce this sound.

The Stomping of Horse Hooves.
Inverted wooden bowls were clapped upon gravel.

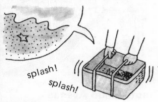

The Splash of Waves
Beans placed in a basket are rythmically rolled to simulate the sound of the waves.

The Patter of Light Rain
An *uchiwa* fan to which beans are attached is waved creating this gentle sound effect.

Double button Model Microphone

Matsuda Model Verocity Microphone

The first television receiver made under contract.

The NHK Broadcasting Science Museum (Located in Atagoyama)
A variety of items related to broadcasting, photos, and old equipment for television and radio broadcasts are on display.

●原宿

HARAJUKU

Harajuku is the strip of land along the east side of the Yamanoté Line station of the same name. After the 1964 Tokyo Olympics, Harajuku became a district noted for fashion with long lines of boutiques and clothing shops.

Harajuku Station
Built in 1924. The design of this structure brings to mind the image of an English station in the countryside.

Omoté-sandō Avenue
This beautiful European-style street lined with *Keyaki* trees has become a gathering place for many young people .

Takeshita Street
A 300 m long road running from the Takeshita exit of Harajuku Station to Meiji Street. Crammed on both sides with boutiques and shops selling small articles, the street is literally overflowing with shoppers and browsers.

Yoyogi Park

Near Harajuku Station just adjacent to Meiji Jingū Shrine (see p. 114) is a large verdant park. In the wide open space covered with forest and grass are walk ways and cycling courses. The entire surface area encompasses 54,000 m^2.

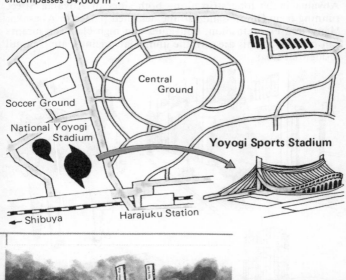

Central Ground

Soccer Ground

National Yoyogi Stadium

Yoyogi Sports Stadium

← Shibuya   Harajuku Station

The area near Yoyogi park becomes a pedestrian mall on Sundays and Holidays. Scores of young teenagers play rock music to the street crowds.

●青山
AOYAMA

Aoyama is the long strip along both sides of Aoyama Street running from Omoté-sando to the detached palace in Akasaka. Many houses of fashion, boutiques and high class restaurants can be seen in this area. In the immediate vicinity are tranquil residential areas.

Children's Castle

The National Center for Children was completed in 1985. It is also known by its more familiar name, "Children's Castle".

Within this structure there is an abundance of open space where children can play freely.

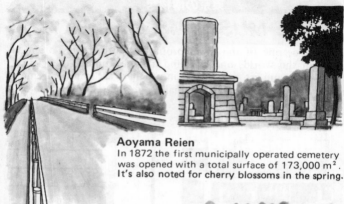

Aoyama Reien

In 1872 the first municipally operated cemetery was opened with a total surface of 173,000 m². It's also noted for cherry blossoms in the spring.

The Nezu Art Museum

Located within a quiet forest in south Aoyama is a museum dedicated to ancient forms of oriental art. Visitors may participate in a tea ceremony held at a tea house in the garden. Appropriate decorum must be observed.

Tea Ceremony Practices

Bow and receive the *chawan* with the right hand, and place it on the palm of the left hand.

Rotate the *chawan* clockwise three times with the right hand.

After drinking the tea rotate the *chawan* counterclockwise, then return it to the host.

東京の博物館

THE MUSEUMS OF TOKYO

In Tokyo, one of the more prominent information-oriented cities in the world, one can find a large number of science, technology and art museums. Among these are some extremely interesting and unusual ones dealing in one particular subject.

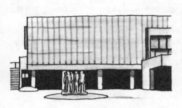

The National Western Art Museum

In the front garden of this museum stands a sculptural piece by Rodin. The museum collection concentrates on 19C French works. (Ueno)

Ōta Memorial Art Museum

This museum was originally started from the collection of *Ōta Seizō*, former president of a big insurance company. Presently, there are over 12,000 pieces of *Ukiyo-é* wood block prints (see p.82) on exhibit.(Harajuku)

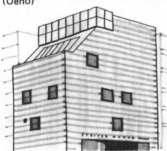

The Stripe House Art Museum

The entire structure of this museum is decorated with beige and brown tiles. This place serves as an artistic spot for contemporary artists to exhibit their works. (Roppongi)

Hōryūji Hōmotsukan

Artisan craftwork of the *Hōryūji* Temple (the oldest temple in all of Japan) in Nara are on display.(Ueno)

The Tokyo National Museum

The first museum in Japan devoted to oriental art and archeological relics. Over 87,500 pieces are kept in storage. (Ueno).

The Japanese Museum of Folk Craft

Established in 1955, this museum contains Porcelain Ware, Dyeing and Weaving, Woodwork, Metalwork, Bamboo Weaving, and other crafts. About 20,000 pieces of work from Japan, Asia, Europe and America are on display.

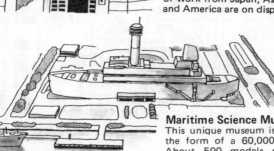

Maritime Science Museum

This unique museum is shaped in the form of a 60,000 ton boat. About 500 models of various ships are on display.

・神宮外苑
JINGŪ GAIEN
• JR Sōbu Line / Near Shinanomachi Sta.

The entire area of this park encompasses 486,000 m². Besides a national sports stadium, it is equipped with facilities for baseball, rugby, tennis and various other athletic events creating a paradise. Lush greenery makes it equally enjoyable for quiet walks in the park.

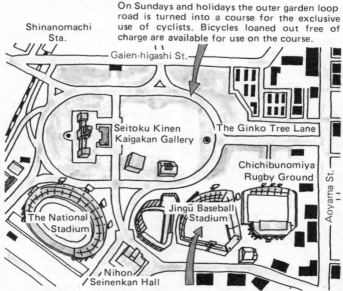

On Sundays and holidays the outer garden loop road is turned into a course for the exclusive use of cyclists. Bicycles loaned out free of charge are available for use on the course.

Shinanomachi Sta.

Gaien-higashi St.

Seitoku Kinen Kaigakan Gallery

The Ginko Tree Lane

Chichibunomiya Rugby Ground

The National Stadium

Jingū Baseball Stadium

Aoyama St.

Nihon Seinenkan Hall

There are also many joggers who run in the nearby area.

The *Jingū* Stadium becomes the scene of fierce competition during the collegiate baseball seasons. (see p.161)

The Ginko Tree Lane

A beautiful 800 m long ginko tree lane leading from the entrance of the picture gallery to Aoyama has become one of the landmarks of the Outer Gardens.

The National Stadium

This stadium built in 1924 is the largest in all of Japan. The main stadium of the Tokyo Olympics, now hosts American football, Soccer and other international events.

Seitoku Kinen Kaigakan, or Meiji Memorial Picture Gallery

The achievements of Emperor *Meiji* and Empress Dowager *Shōken* (see p. 114) are depicted in Japanese paintings. There are also 80 foreign and Japanese paintings on display. In addition to the ginko tree lane this building is another landmark of the Outer Gardens.

· 新宿
SHINJUKU

Shinjuku Station handles the largest number of train passengers in all of Japan. This played a major role in the evolution of the surrounding area into one of the most prominent entertainment districts of Tokyo. Skyscrapers cluster the west end area in contrast to wide underground shopping centers.

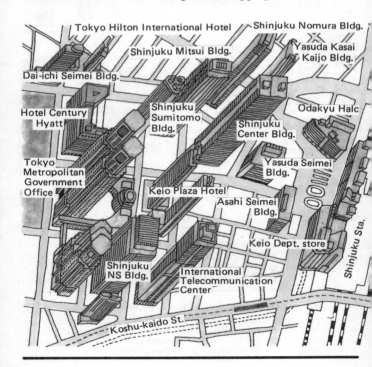

Tokyo Hilton International Hotel

Shinjuku Nomura Bldg.

Shinjuku Mitsui Bldg.

Yasuda Kasai Kaijo Bldg.

Dai-ichi Seimei Bldg.

Odakyu Halc

Hotel Century Hyatt

Shinjuku Sumitomo Bldg.

Shinjuku Center Bldg.

Yasuda Seimei Bldg.

Tokyo Metropolitan Government Office

Keio Plaza Hotel

Asahi Seimei Bldg.

Keio Dept. store

Shinjuku NS Bldg.

International Telecommunication Center

Shinjuku Sta.

Koshu-kaido St.

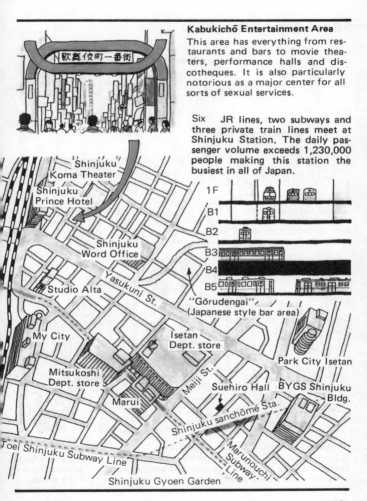

Kabukichō Entertainment Area

This area has everything from restaurants and bars to movie theaters, performance halls and discotheques. It is also particularly notorious as a major center for all sorts of sexual services.

Six JR lines, two subways and three private train lines meet at Shinjuku Station. The daily passenger volume exceeds 1,230,000 people making this station the busiest in all of Japan.

"Shinjuku" Koma Theater

Shinjuku Prince Hotel

Shinjuku Word Office

Yasukuni St.

Studio Alta

My City

Mitsukoshi Dept. store

Marui

1F
B1
B2
B3
B4
B5

"Gōrudengai" (Japanese style bar area)

Isetan Dept. store

Park City Isetan

Meiji St.

Suehiro Hall

BYGS Shinjuku Bldg.

Shinjuku sanchōmé Sta.

Toei Shinjuku Subway Line

Marunouchi Subway Line

Shinjuku Gyoen Garden

Sightseeing Spots in Shinjuku

Studio Alta
A huge video screen on the side of this building catches the eye as soon as one comes out of the east exit of Shinjuku Station.

Fashion, restaurants, and information (the three things most valued by young people in Japan) are available in this building. Live broadcasts are often held within the premises of Studio Alta.

Shinjuku Discount Camera District
Shinjuku is also well known for the many discount camera shops located in the area. At both the east and west exits of the station, flashy signs and enthusiastic salesmen try to draw customers into the shops.

Suehiro Hall

This famous variety theater in the Shinjuku area features *Rakugo* performance.

Shinjuku Gyoen Garden

An enormous 581,00 m² garden, originally attached to the Imperial household, harmonizes the influences from French Restoration, English countryside and Japanese Traditional style gardens.

Underground Shopping Centers

As the main train terminals in Tokyo grew, the underground shopping centers kept pace accordingly. The long and wide shopping center underneath Shinjuku Station is no exception. The passageways between the east and west exits served as the central point for the evolution in opposite directions of this shopping street.

THE SKYSCRAPERS OF TOKYO

On the west side of the Shinjuku Station area 14 skyscrapers were constructed in the space of about 20 years. It has now become a very important office area. In size, all of them out-

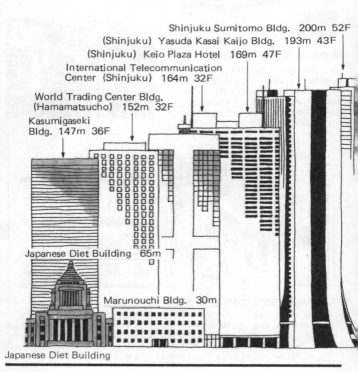

Shinjuku Sumitomo Bldg. 200m 52F
(Shinjuku) Yasuda Kasai Kaijo Bldg. 193m 43F
(Shinjuku) Keio Plaza Hotel 169m 47F
International Telecommunication Center (Shinjuku) 164m 32F
World Trading Center Bldg. (Hamamatsucho) 152m 32F
Kasumigaseki Bldg. 147m 36F
Japanese Diet Building 65m
Marunouchi Bldg. 30m

Japanese Diet Building

rank the Kasumigaseki Building (see p. 96), the very first skyscraper in Japan. Since earthquakes occur regularly in Japan, it is crucial that extremely rigid standards of quality and the application of the very latest technical advances preceed the construction of skyscrapers.

Tokyo Metropolitan Government Office (Shinjuku) 243m 48F
(Ikebukuro) Sunshine 60 240m 60F
Shinjuku Center Bldg. 216m 54F
Shinjuku Mitsui Bldg. 212m 55F
Shinjuku Nomura
Bldg. 210m 50F

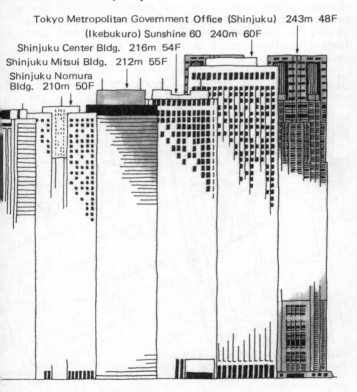

IKEBUKURO

Ikebukuro is a district which has undergone significant expansion since the start of the Meiji period in 1868. It is now a thriving, vibrant commercial area attracting as many young people as Shibuya and Shinjuku. The streets in the immediate vicinity of the station are lined with department stores, fashion buildings, movie theaters, and eating and drinking spots.

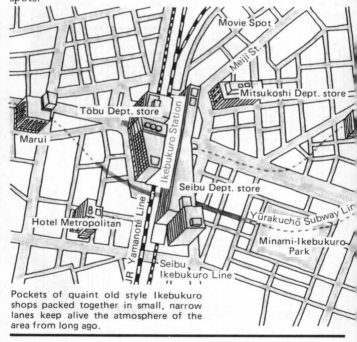

Pockets of quaint old style Ikebukuro shops packed together in small, narrow lanes keep alive the atmosphere of the area from long ago.

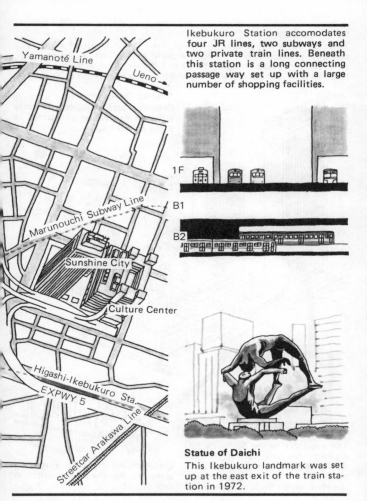

Ikebukuro Station accomodates four JR lines, two subways and two private train lines. Beneath this station is a long connecting passage way set up with a large number of shopping facilities.

Yamanoté Line

Ueno →

Marunouchi Subway Line

Sunshine City

Culture Center

Higashi-Ikebukuro Sta.

EXPWY 5

Streetcar Arakawa Line

1F

B1

B2

Statue of Daichi

This Ikebukuro landmark was set up at the east exit of the train station in 1972.

Sunshine City

This 60 story skyscraper is one of the highest in all of Asia. The complex is comprised of offices, a performance hall, an art museum, an aquarium, shopping malls, parks and hotels. Soon after it's completion in 1980, it became one of the major points of interest in Tokyo.

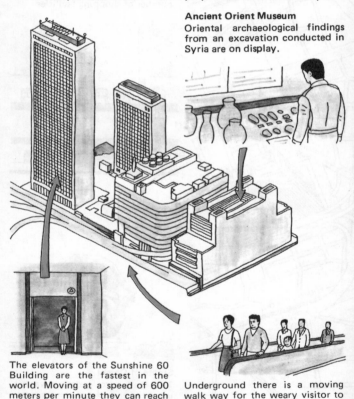

Ancient Orient Museum

Oriental archaeological findings from an excavation conducted in Syria are on display.

The elevators of the Sunshine 60 Building are the fastest in the world. Moving at a speed of 600 meters per minute they can reach the observation deck in 35 seconds.

Underground there is a moving walk way for the weary visitor to ride on.

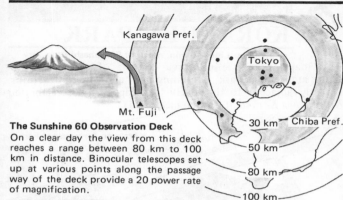

The Sunshine 60 Observation Deck

On a clear day the view from this deck reaches a range between 80 km to 100 km in distance. Binocular telescopes set up at various points along the passage way of the deck provide a 20 power rate of magnification.

The Message Water Fountain

Messages and the time are displayed in the component jets of water forming this fountain.

The Sunshine International Aquarium

The first aquarium of its kind in the world set up in a high rise structure. The lovely illuminated tints and hues of over 20,000 fish from 400 different species are on exhibit.

●後楽園
KŌRAKUEN PARK

● JR Sōbu Line / 5 min. north of Suidōbashi Sta.

This major urban leisure area consists of a baseball stadium, amusement park, swimming pool and other attractions. Directly adjacent to the lovely landscapes of the celebrated *Koishikawa Kōrakuen* Garden (see p. 74).

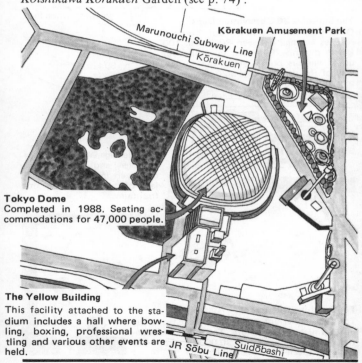

Kōrakuen Amusement Park

Marunouchi Subway Line

Kōrakuen

Tokyo Dome
Completed in 1988. Seating accommodations for 47,000 people.

The Yellow Building
This facility attached to the stadium includes a hall where bowling, boxing, professional wrestling and various other events are held.

JR Sōbu Line

Suidōbashi

Kōrakuen Amusement Park

Opened in 1955, this urban amusement park has 27 rides in all . Over 3 million people visit the park annually.

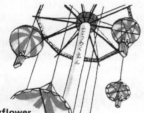

Skyflower

This ride simulates the thrill of a parachute fall from 70 m above the ground.

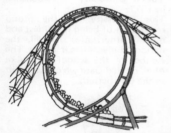

Kōrakuen Tower

This slowly revolving observation deck rises to a height of 100 m in the air.

The Boomerang

A forward and backward moving roller coaster complete with loops.

Tokyo Dome (Big Egg)

Tokyo Dome is the first stadium in Japan to be covered by a roof. Besides baseball many other games such as soccer and football will be held.

THE UNVERSITIES OF TOKYO

Tokyo is also noted as a great center of education in Japan with approximately 250 universities. There are many famous universities with a long history dating back to the Meiji period. Among these are some highly reputable ones whose names have been adopted by the train stations serving them and in some cases by the neighboring residential areas.

Akamon

Tokyo University — Established in 1877.

This university has the proud reputation of being the oldest and most authoritative of all the national universities in Japan. The symbol of the school is its *Aka mon,* or Red Gate which was built in the Edo period.

Keiō Gijuku University — Established in 1858.

This university is particularly noted for its founder, *Fukuzawa Yukichi*, an influential figure of the Meiji period. His likeness appears on the 10,000 yen bill.

Waseda University — Established in 1882.

This school has been known for the great importance it attached to an old school notion called *"Bankara"*.

The Tokyo Big Six Universities

One of the divisions of the University Baseball Competition Leagues consists of the following group: *Waseda, Keiō, Tokyo, Hōsei, Meiji,* and *Rikkyō*. They are commonly referred to as the Tokyo Big Six Universities. The *Jingū* Stadium located in Aoyama is renowned as the mecca for collegiate baseball competition. Annual league competition events are held there in the spring and autumn.

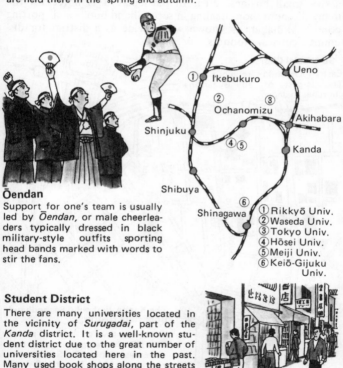

Ōendan

Support for one's team is usually led by *Ōendan*, or male cheerleaders typically dressed in black military-style outfits sporting head bands marked with words to stir the fans.

① Rikkyō Univ.
② Waseda Univ.
③ Tokyo Univ.
④ Hōsei Univ.
⑤ Meiji Univ.
⑥ Keiō-Gijuku Univ.

Student District

There are many universities located in the vicinity of *Surugadai*, part of the *Kanda* district. It is a well-known student district due to the great number of universities located here in the past. Many used book shops along the streets are always crowded with large numbers of college students.

161

KANDA·AKIHABARA

Kanda was an area which prospered with the arrival of many craftsmen and merchants to Edo city. At present it is still an active small business area. In particular it is noted for the many discount shops dealing in secondhand books and sporting goods. Akihabara is known world wide as a district for discount electrical products.

St. Nicolai Church

Eastern Orthodox religious Sect. The largest of all Byzantine churches in Japan.

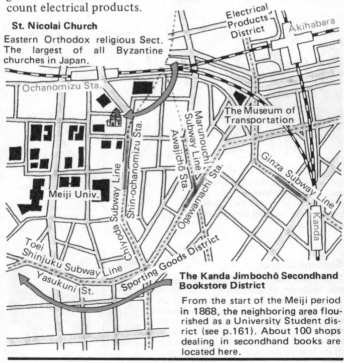

Electrical Products District

Akihabara

The Museum of Transportation

Ochanomizu Sta.

Chiyoda Subway Line

Shin-ochanomizu Sta.

Marunouchi Subway Line

Awajichō Sta.

Ogawamachi Sta.

Ginza Subway Line

Kanda

Meiji Univ.

Toei Shinjuku Subway Line

Yasukuni St.

Sporting Goods District

The Kanda Jimbochō Secondhand Bookstore District

From the start of the Meiji period in 1868, the neighboring area flourished as a University Student district (see p.161). About 100 shops dealing in secondhand books are located here.

162

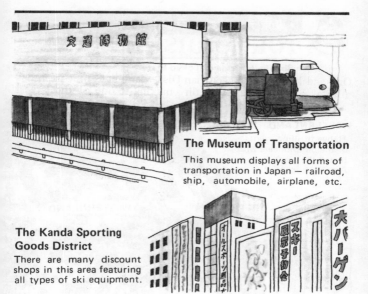

The Museum of Transportation

This museum displays all forms of transportation in Japan — railroad, ship, automobile, airplane, etc.

The Kanda Sporting Goods District

There are many discount shops in this area featuring all types of ski equipment.

The Akihabara Electrical Products District

There are about 600 shops in the Akihabara area dealing in a wide assortment of electrical goods and related supplies. Discounts range from 10% to 50% The bright colored flashing lights and blaring sounds of the vast array of shops are an exciting experience for the first time visitor.

163

●東京ディズニーランド
TOKYO DISNEYLAND ®

● 35 min. bus ride of Tokyo Sta.

One and half times bigger than Disneyland in California, it has
a total surface area of 82.6h , making it one of the largest

WESTERNLAND

Relive thrilling events
of the old pioneers who
tamed the great
American frontier.

WESTERNLAND

ADVENTURELAND

ADVENTURELAND

Excitement awaits you
at every turn as you
explore the great
tropical unknowns in
search of exotic
cultures.

WORLD BAZAAR

The good old days at the turn of the century!
You'll find them here in this nostalgic small
town lined with shops chock-full of souvenirs
and goodies that take you back to the days of
yesteryear.

theme parks in the world. The interior is completely modeled after its American counterpart with five different theme lands. Over 10 million people visit this amusement area annually.

FANTASYLAND

All of your favorite characters from fairy tales and movies are here to take young and old alike back to this magical land of enchantment and dreams.

TOMORROWLAND

Reach for a star on a journey through time and space as you chart a celestial course through the Milkyway.

HANEDA AIRPORT

● **Tokyo Monorail / 5 min. of Haneda Sta.**

First opened in 1931, it became Tokyo International Airport in 1952. With the completion of the New Tokyo International Airport in Narita in 1978, almost all the international flights were rerouted to the new airport with the exception of a few international flights. Haneda airport has now become a center widely used for domestic service.

Anamori Inari Branch Shrine
Formerly located within the airport site. Although this shrine was transferred at the time of the expansion of runway facilities, a small branch shrine was left behind on the roof of the terminal building in the hope of insuring airport safety.

A connecting monorail service running to the airport is conveniently located at the JR Hamamatsuchō Station. (A 15 minute ride along this 13.1 km track).

Useful Information

Japanese-style Inns

Although there are many western style hotels in Tokyo, *Ryokan*, or Japanese style inns, are a wounderful change of pace for those wishing to experience warm Japanese hospitality in a truly traditional setting.

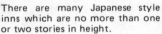

There are many Japanese style inns which are no more than one or two stories in height.

Maids dressed in *kimono* greet guests at the entrance upon arrival. Shoes are removed here and slippers are put on in their place.

Guest sleeping quarters are furnished with *tatami* mat floors. Slippers are removed at the entrance. At night *futon*, or traditional Japanese style floor bedding is laid out for the guests to sleep on.

Economy Inns

In Tokyo, various reasonably priced inns geared toward the international tourist are available for those wishing to stay in Tokyo. Somewhat small sized capsule hotels occasionally used by Japanese people on business trips are also available.

Youth Hostels
A large scale youth hostel has the foreign visitor in mind, offering the same type of facilities as those in hotels.

Low Priced Japanese-style Inn
Catering especially to the international visitor to Japan, these are the places where any Japanese on a limited budget would stay.

Capsule Hotel
One person rooms arranged into small package type facilities. A "no frills" hotel providing nothing more than the bare essentials.

Currency

In Japan at present, six kinds of coins and three denominations of banknotes are used.

1,000yen

5,000yen

10,000yen

1yen 5yen 10yen 50yen 100yen

500yen

Ten and one hundred yen coins are the most commonly used. One and five yen pieces are also used since consumption tax was introduced.

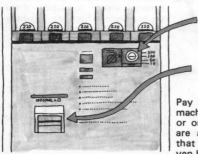

100yen

10yen 50yen 500yen

1000円 1,000yen

Pay telephones and vending machines usually take either ten or one hundred yen coins. There are also some vending machines that will accept a one thousand yen bill.

170

Public Telephones

Many public telephones are conveniently located near stations and department stores and on the streets. The various functions and uses of these telephones are marked by six color categories : red, pink, green, gray, blue and yellow.

Green telephones
These phones will accept a magnetic card as well as coins.

Yellow telephones
These coins use ten and one hundred yen coins for toll and long distance calls.

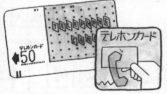

Telephone Cards
Since calls within Tokyo cost 10 yen for each three minutes, these magnetic cards are particularly useful when speaking for long period of time. Usually sold at shops near the green phones.

USEFUL PHONE NUMBERS

Police. 110
Fire Department, Ambulance
. . . . 119
Time 117
Weather 177
Directory Assistance in Tokyo
and other areas 104
Call Collect 106
Narita Flight Information
. . . . 0476-32-2800
Operator Assisted Calls. . .0051
Tourist Information Center
. . . . 3502-1461
Teletourist Service . 3503-2911

Toilet Facilities

The design of Japanese squat type and Western sit down type toilets are completely different. The correct manner of use may appear a little confusing at first to the international traveller. But, unlike sit down toilets, the Japanese consider the squat-type quite hygienic since there is never any direct contact with the toilet fixtures.

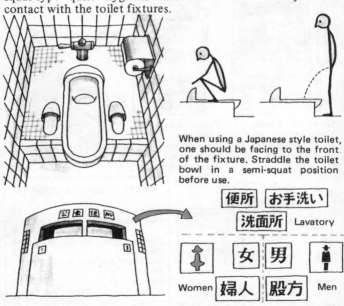

When using a Japanese style toilet, one should be facing to the front of the fixture. Straddle the toilet bowl in a semi-squat position before use.

便所	お手洗い

洗面所 Lavatory

	女	男	
Women	婦人	殿方	Men

Toilets in train stations and parks usually provide neither paper towels nor toilet paper. Therefore it would always be wise to carry a handkerchief to wipe one's hands and a packet of tissue paper for use in public facilities.

Public Baths

Public baths are set up as washing facilities for those dwellings not equipped with bathtubs or showers. In the past, the public bath was an extremely popular place for socializing with neighbors and friends.

The interior bathing facilities are divided into segregated areas for men and women. The bathtubs themselves are much bigger than those used in regular households.

On the wall behind the bath itself, there is usually a painting of a Japanese scene.

The bath area

In a Japanese bath it is extremely important to remember that scrubbing and washing with soap are always done OUTSIDE of the bath tub. Soap is rinsed off by dousing oneself with water poured into a small bucket. The function of the bathtub is to warm the body and serve as a relaxing natural way to relieve aches and pains brought on by normal everyday stress and exertion.

173

Pachinko Game Parlors

Pachinko is a distinctively Japanese type of game. In design it vaguely ressembles a vertical version of a pinball machine. The objective is to drop a ball into holes that release fixed numbers of balls from within.

The outside of a *pachinko* parlor is characterized by the blaring sound of music used to attrack people inside.

Practically all *pachinko* machines are operated by electric powered flippers used to aim the balls into the holes.

When one has finished the play, the balls are collected and can be exchanged for non-cash prizes.

Within the city there are many important directional and informational signs posted. Although almost all are written in Japanese, many are easy to understand using the international sign system adopted by most countries throughout the world. The following are a list of the ones most commonly appearing in Japan.

非常口 EXIT

EMERGENCY EXIT

出口 EXIT

入口 ENTRANCE

みどりの窓口

RESERVATIONS (for trains — also called "Green Window")

駐車場 PARKING

禁煙 NO SMOKING

危険 DANGER

地下鉄 SUBWAY

大人 ADULT

小人 CHILD

TAXI
タクシー
のりば

TAXIS

CROSSWALK SIGNAL

POST BOX

JR and Subways in Tokyo

Kotaké-mukaihara

Nishi-sugamo

Kanamechō

Ōtsuka

Senkawa

Sugamo

Shin-sakuradai

Ikebukuro

Shin-ōtsuka

Sengoku

Mejiro

Higashi-ikebukuro

Myōgadani

Takadanobaba

Gokokuji

Edogawabashi

Ochiai

Waseda

Kagurazaka

Shin-ōkubo

Akebonobashi

Ichigaya

Nakano

Ōkubo

Higashi-Nakano

Shinjuku

Shinjukugyoen-maé

Nakanosakaué

Shinjuku-sanchōme

Yotsuya

Yotsuya-sanchōmé

JR Yamanoté Line

Kōjimachi

Yoyogi

JR Chūō Line

Nagatachō

Yoyogi-uehara

Shinanomachi

Akasaka-mitsuke

Sendagaya

Yoyogi-kōen

Aoyamaitchōmé

Harajuku

Meiji-jingū-maé

Gaienmaé

Akasaka

Shibuya

Omoté-sandō

Nogizaka

Roppongi

Ebisu

Hiro-o

Kamiyachō

Nakameguro

Meguro

Takanawadai

Togoshi

Gotanda

Sengaku

Nakanobu

Ōsaki

Shinagawa

Komagome　Tabata　JR Jōban Line　Machiya　Kita-senju
　　　　　　　　　　　　　Minami-senju
Hakusan　　Nishi-nippori　Mikawashima　Minami-senju
Sendagi　　　Nippori　　Minowa　　　Oshiagé
Kasuga　Nezu　Uguisudani　Iriya　Honjo
　Kōrakuen　Yushima　Inarichō　Asakusa　azumabashi
Iidabashi　Hongōsanchōmé　Ueno　Tawaramachi
Suidōbashi　Ueno-hirokōji　Nakaokachimachi　Kuramaé
Jimbōchō　Ochanomizu　Okachimachi
Kudanshita　Shin-ochanomizu　Akihabara　JR Sōbu Line
Hanzōmon　Ogawamachi　Ryōgoku　Kinshichō
Takebashi　Awajichō
Sakuradamon　Ōtemachi　Asakusabashi
Kokkai-gijidōmaé　Nijūbashimaé　Iwamotochō　Bakurochō
Kasumigaseki　Kanda　Higashi-nihombashi
Uchisaiwaichō　Hibiya　Tōkyō　Shin-　Bakuroyokoyama
Toranomon　Yūrakuchō　nihombashi　Hamachō
　Shimbashi　Kodemmachō
Daimon　Ginza-　Mitsukoshimaé　Edobashi　Morishita
Onari-　itchōmé　Nihombashi　Ningyōchō
mon　Hamamatsuchō　Kyōbashi　Suitengūmaé
Hibakōen　Ginza　Takarachō　Kayabachō
　　Higashi-ginza　Shintomichō　Monzen-nakachō
Mita　Higashi-ginza　Hatchōbori
Tamachi　Tsukiji　Tsukishima　Kiba

Ginza Subway Line	Yūrakuchō Subway Line
Marunouchi Subway Line	Toei Asakusa Subway Line
Hibiya Subway Line	Toei Mita Subway Line
Tōzai Subway Line	Toei Shinjuku Subway Line
Chiyoda Subway Line	Hanzōmon Subway Line

Mass Transit Systems

Tokyo is a city well known worldwide for its highly developed train systems. Once international travellers have learned how to handle them, like many Tokyoites, they too will be able to benefit from this safe, convenient and highly reliable form of transportation.

Yamanoté Line — green
Keihin-Tōhoku Line — blue
Chūō Line — orange
Sōbu Line — yellow

JR
The carriages of the major train lines are color coded for easy recognition and use.

Subways
The Tokyo subways cover almost every area in the city. This complex of lines is interlinked at various cross points.

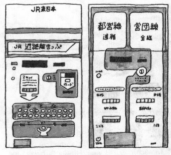

All tickets for JR Railways and subway trains are sold in vending machines.

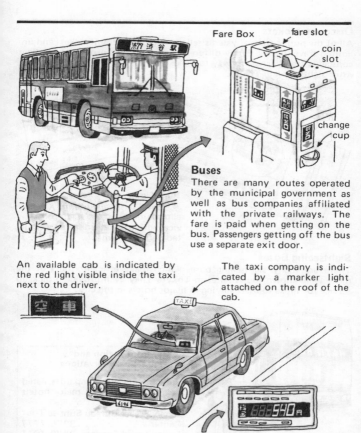

Fare Box — fare slot, coin slot, change cup

Buses

There are many routes operated by the municipal government as well as bus companies affiliated with the private railways. The fare is paid when getting on the bus. Passengers getting off the bus use a separate exit door.

An available cab is indicated by the red light visible inside the taxi next to the driver.

空車

The taxi company is indicated by a marker light attached on the roof of the cab.

Taxis

There are always lots of taxis running on the streets of Tokyo. All are clean and maintained in good working order.

The fare calculated by the distance and time involved is displayed on a meter. An increased night rate goes into effect from **10:00 p.m.** until **6:00 a.m.**

Discount Tickets

All of the public transit systems sell easy to use discount tickets and un-limited travel passes. These different ticket options provide the budget conscious traveller with a way to make the best use of his or her money while sightseeing in Tokyo.

Furī Kippu

A travel pass called *"Furī Kippu"* allows unlimited use of transit service within a set zone for a limited period of time.

Sightseeing Buses

There are many sightseeing buses which make efficient tours of the more well known tourist sites in Tokyo. They even provide a pick up service for those tourists staying in major hotels in the city.

● **For information and Reservations**

Call any of the companies listed below or go to any major hotels in the city.

Japan Travel Bureau Sunrise Tour Center 3276-7777
Fujita Travel Service . 3573-1011
Hankyu Express International. 3508-0129
Hato Bus. 3435-6081
Japan Gray Line. . . . 3436-6881

Tokyo has been used as both the setting and the subject of many movies. A few of the movies representative of the various themes dealing with life and events in Tokyo from Edo period up to modern times are presented here.

"Bakumatsu Taiyōden", directed by Kawashima Yūzō.
A cinematic work dramatizing some of the incidents taken from *Rakugo* stories, the lively atmosphere of the Shinagawa area at the end of the Edo period is re-created in this film.

"Tokyo Story", directed by Ozu Yasujirō.
This movie uses the Tokyo of the latter half of the 1940's as the setting. Considered an accomplished work in its subdued portrayal of events, this movie has won the acclaim of critics both at home and abroad.

"No yōnamono", directed by Morita Yoshimitsu.
A rising figure in the vanguard of a new generation of Japanese films directors, Morita Yoshimitsu made his debut as a director with this work. The *Shitamachi* old downtown area of Tokyo is cleverly presented through the actions of the hero of this story, a *Rakugo* artist.

181

Festivals and Annual Events in Tokyo

● January

1-7: Hatsumōdé/Meiji-jingū Shrine and many other temples and shrines.
People pay their first visit of the year to pray for health and happiness in the coming year.

2: Commoners visit to The Imperial Palace (P.90)

6: Shōbō Dezomeshiki or The Fire Fighter's New Year Parade/Harumi Pier (P.68)

8: Dondoyaki/Torigoé Shrine/ Pine branches and other decorations used at New Year's are burned.

● February

3 or 4: Setsubun-é/Sannō Hié-jinja Shrine and all other temples and shrines/The men and women born during that particular year of the Chinese astrological calendar throw beans at devils to bring about good fortune.

8: Harikuyō/Awashimadō (Sensōji Temple) and all other temples and shrines (P.24)

25 to March 15: Shiraumé Matsuri, or Plum Festival/Yushima-tenjin Shrine/Tea ceremony and performances are presented under white plum blossoms.

● March

18: Asakusa Kannon Jigen-é/Sensōji Temple/*Kinryū-no-mai* is performed. (P.21)

● April

1-15: Sakura Matsuri, or Cherry Blossom Festival/Ueno Park/During this annual event people take in the cherry blossom sights with song and drink. *(Hanami,* see P.45)

● May

11-15: Kanda Festival/Kanda-myōjin Shrine/This festival is one of Tokyo's three big festivals. On the 12th, the town-*mikoshi* enter the shrine one after the other, about 70 in all.

Mid-May: Sanja Festival/Asakusa Shrine (P.30)

● June

10-16: Sannō Festival/Sannō Hié Shrine (P.79)

The 2nd Sunday:Torigoé Night Festival/Torigoé Shrine/The magnificent evening spectacle of *mikoshi* covered with lighted paper lanterns at night.

- **July**

6-8: **Asagao-Ichi, or Morning-Glory Market/Iriya Kishibojin Temple** (P.27)

9-10: **Hōzuki-Ichi/Sensōji Temple** (P.26)

Mid-July to mid-August: **Edo Shumi Nōryō Taikai/Shinobazu Pond in Ueno Park**/Various performances are held.

The last Saturday: **Sumida River Firework/The banks of the Sumida River** (P.35)

- **August**

4-6: **Sumiyoshi-jinja reisai / Sumiyoshi Shrine** /Procession of 6 *mikoshi* invoking protection from illness. Grappling with a giant statue of a lion.

4-6: **Crockery Market/Ningyōcho commercial district** (P.58)/Crockery is sold at rock-bottom prices.

- **September**

Early September: **Tsukimi-no-Kai, or Moon Viewing Ceremony/Mukō-jima Hyakkaen Garden** (P.60)/ Event to admire the evening moon.

11-21: **Daradara Festival/Shiba-Daijingū Shrine**/Spread over so many days it is called dara-dara or sluggish. Well known for the ginger market.

20-21: **Nezu-gongen Matsuri or Nezu Shrine Annual Festival/Nezu-gongen Shrine**/*Sengan mikoshi* are pulled through the town with festival floats.

- **October**

19-20: **Bettara-Ichi/Takarada Shrine**/A *daikon* (white raddish) condiment called *bettara-zuké* is sold.

30 to November 3: **Meiji-jingū Shrine Annual Festival/Meiji-jingū Shrine** (P.116)/Dances, *Noh,* music, *Yabusamé* and archery offered.

- **November**

Tori-no-hi: Tori-no-Ichi/Ōtori Shrine or any other shrines (P.84) **Mid to late November: Chrysanthemum Show/Shinjuku Gyoen Park**

- **December**

17-19: **Hagoita-Ichi, or Battledore Market/Sensōji Temple** (P.26)

《INDEX》

189

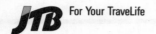

For Your TraveLife

英文 **日本絵とき事典 7**

ILLUSTRATED

A LOOK INTO TOKYO

初 版 発 行 1986年7月1日
改訂6版 1991年7月10日
(Jul. 10, 1991 6th edition)

編 集 人 宮崎 裕
発 行 人 岩田光正
発 行 所 JTB日本交通公社出版事業局
〒150 東京都渋谷区道玄坂1-10-8 渋谷野村ビル7階
印 刷 所 交通印刷株式会社

─────────────────────────

● スタッフ

企画・編集 JTB出版事業局 編集二部
外語図書編集 担当編集長 黒澤明夫
編集部直通 ☎03-3477-9566
取材・編集協力 株式会社 アーバン・トランスレーション
イ ラ ス ト 松下正己
表紙デザイン 東 芳純
翻 訳 Arnold Ross Falvo

─────────────────────────

● JTB発行図書のご注文は
JTB出版販売センター
〒150 東京都渋谷区道玄坂1-10-8 渋谷野村ビル7階 ☎03-3477-9588
● 広告のお問合せは
JTB出版事業局広告課 ☎03-3477-9531

913811 712091
ISBN4-533-00664-7